HEAVEN
at Home

HEAVEN
at Home

Establishing and Enjoying a Peaceful Home

GINGER PLOWMAN

Shepherd Press
Wapwallopen, Pennsylvania

To my family

Jim, Wesley, and Alex
You fill our home with love, laughter,
and the richest of blessings

Contents

Acknowledgements

WITH ALL MY HEART, I'd like to thank:

My incredible husband, Jim—I could not have written this book without your encouragement and support. You are truly the most amazing man I've ever known. I love you.

My wonderful children, Wesley and Alex—You two are my greatest blessings. You never complained, but spurred me on during endless hours of writing. I am so proud of you both for opening your lives and allowing me to share personal family stories for the glory of God and the encouragement of others.

Aaron Tripp—I cannot say enough. Gospel hope forms the backbone of this book because of your input. You caused me to take a deeper look at the grace of God and coached me in shaping a weak manuscript that missed the mark in many ways into a more Christ-centered presentation of the gospel. You have greatly influenced this book as well as my life. Thank you, my friend.

Tedd Tripp—I believe God created you with an extra dose of patience in preparation for dealing with this hard-headed author. Thank you for not giving up on me in spite of my arguing, for encouraging me to grow in the wisdom of the Lord, and, *I can't believe*

I'm saying this, for requiring me to rewrite Heaven at Home THREE times. Yes, you were right; it is a better book because of it.

Ruth Younts—In talking about your editorial skills, your husband once wrote to me, "She has a rare combination of grammatical, literary and theological skills which are all excellent." I agree. Thank you for your valuable investment.

Rick Irvin—Sweet Rick. You spent countless hours looking at cover design, content, layout, and who knows what else in order for everything to be just right. Thank you for polishing the apple.

Valerie Shepard—The wisdom you share in chapter 15 is invaluable. Your honesty and transparency will point many frustrated, discouraged women to the Giver of Peace.

Matt Hawkins—One of your insightful sermons motivated me to write chapter 9. Much of the content in this chapter resulted from what I learned under your teaching.

Phil Swearengin—The survey you orchestrated for Sunday school classes was beneficial to this book. Thank you for taking time to help.

Pre-publication readers—Many thanks to all of you who read through the manuscript and offered helpful suggestions: Chuck and Bonnie Ferrell, Lee and Thelma Plowman, Cliff and Toma Knight, Gina Ferrell, Lisa O'Quinn, Rebecca Ingram Powell, Julie Daum, Tracey Youngblood, Vince and Paula Swanson, Jami Sims, JJ and Renee Swope, and Pam Shattuck. Your comments, critiques, and advice helped to iron out the wrinkles.

Deborah Stabler—My grammar Nazi. Oh, the stories you could tell!

Linda Currie—What a blessing you have been since coming on staff! I don't know how I ever survived without you. Thank you for carrying so much of the load. Because of your servant's heart, I am able to minister more effectively.

Al Roland—If I ever became computer savvy, who would interrupt your concentration at work and harass you with late night phone calls? What are friends for? You're always there when I need you. Thanks.

My prayer team—I would have never made it to the finish line without your petitioning and interceding on my behalf. There is no doubt in my mind that God hears and answers the prayers of the Saints. Thank you for standing in the gap for me as I run the race.

My Savior and Lord, Jesus Christ—You are the Way, the Truth, the Life, and the Almighty *Giver of Peace*. Thank you for making yourself known to me nineteen years ago. May you be glorified through this book.

Introduction

W͟H͟E͟N I W͟A͟S S͟E͟R͟V͟I͟N͟G what seemed like a life sentence in high school, Friday nights were like cashing in a get-out-of-jail-free card. Oh, the freedom my friends and I felt as the final bell sounded at 3:00. We would begin our weekend parole by crowding in front of one mirror. With giggles, we passed around the cotton candy lip-gloss, drenched ourselves in way too much perfume and moussed up our over-permed "big hair." Then all five of us would pile into my two-seater sports car (top down, of course) and cruise from one teenage hangout to the other. Life was good.

We would crank up the radio to a volume that should be illegal and rock to the beat as we sang with the Go-Go Girls, *Ooooh, baby do ya know what that's worth? Oooooh, heaven is a place on earth.*

Isn't that just what we all crave? No, not cruising around in an over-crowded sports car. I'm talking about heavenly paradise. Don't we all long to dwell in perfect peace, constant contentment, and holy harmony? If someone's serving up a little heaven, who wouldn't want a slice? Unfortunately, heaven itself doesn't exist on earth. Heaven is the one and only perfect place because it is the home of the one and only perfect God. You won't find anyone strolling down the streets of gold beyond the crystal sea on this side of glory.

However, those who seek to be like Jesus and follow him whole-heartedly can experience an appetizer of heaven while here on earth. I may not be able to have the whole pie but I'd certainly rather have a slice than nothing at all.

Webster's dictionary describes home as "the physical structure within which one lives." I say home is much more than that. It's a candle in the window, a cup of hot chocolate on a cold night, a band-aid on a boo-boo, laughter around the kitchen table, a cool damp cloth on a fevered forehead, the crackling of a fire, a good movie with a bowl of buttered popcorn, the smell of mom's chicken casserole, a warm bubble bath, a cozy bed, and the soothing sound of raindrops on a roof.

Home is where we can kick off our shoes, throw on an old cotton T-shirt, and flop down on the couch. Home is a haven where energy is restored, spirits are renewed, and love resides. It's a place where dreams are nurtured, plans are made, and the best of life is lived. Home is where the heart is.

Your childhood memories may not be so fond. Maybe you looked forward to leaving home as soon as possible. Perhaps home triggers feelings of anger, bitterness, or even fear. If so, let the light of Jesus' healing shine through your hurt and brighten your home. May you break the pattern of turmoil and create a pleasant home of harmony.

Jesus longs for us to bask in the blessings of peace and to dwell together in unity. He desires that we practice love, joy, peace, patience, kindness, goodness, faithfulness, gentleness, and self-control (Galatians 5:22–23) in our earthly residence in preparation for the eternal, glorious mansions he has prepared for us in heaven. He longs for us to live in such a way that he is glorified.

How can we glorify God? Our obedience shows God's greatness to others. By living in obedience to his commands we display his power and love and mercy. We demonstrate to the world how good his righteous ways are. Our highest motive must be to be a blessing to God.

Remember, as you read through this book, that being better wives, moms and homemakers does not make us more worthy of God's love. My friend Aaron put it this way, "Our acceptance before God is not based on our conformity to human standards or our perfect obedience. Jesus has obeyed in our place and has paid the full penalty for our disobedience. There is nothing left, either in terms of obedience or judgment, for us to get credit for. We are not justified on the basis of our successful obedience. We must hold this truth continually before ourselves lest we become prideful in our successes or defeated in our failures. We must have the glorious message of the gospel be the lens through which we see all of life."

We honor and obey Jesus not for the good it brings us (although good comes), but to give him pleasure through a worshipful life. It will be tempting to read this book with the mindset of, "What steps must I take in order to have a peaceful home? How can I be a happier, more fulfilled Christian?" I urge you to read this book with the mindset of, "Although there is nothing I can do to earn righteousness and acceptance, how can I radiate the peace of Christ so that his character might be glorified in and through me? How can I bless God in the way I treat my family? How can my mind be transformed that I might become more pleasing to Jesus?"

You see, establishing and enjoying a peaceful home is for God's glory. A Christ-centered home does result in a more productive, more fulfilling life, but only because it is first focused on pleasing Christ. It is a way to fulfill the very purpose for which we were created—to worship God in all we do.

Let us delight in establishing a haven in which our loved ones can rest and laugh and cry and love. Let us bless God's heart as we set to cleaning, organizing, cooking and creating an atmosphere of warmth, beauty and hopefulness. Let us seek to make God famous as we explore together the makings of a heavenly home!

—Ginger Plowman

PART ONE

Home is Heavenly

When the Woman is Happy

Delighting in Who You Are

WE'VE ALL HEARD THE SAYING, "If Mama ain't happy, ain't nobody happy." I'm sure we have all experienced the truth of it as well. The woman sets the ambiance of the home. If Mom delights in the role that God has ordained her to fill, she sets the stage for the other family members to do the same. When Mom is mom it's easier for Dad to be dad and children to be children.

Mom has the power to make or break the family order. Just as removing one block from a Jinga™ tower causes the tower to come crashing down into a heap, so can a mother, who removes herself from her God-given position in the family, cause the foundation of that family to collapse.

If Mom is uptight and stressed-out over the responsibilities and realities of life, her tension will rub off on the attitudes of her family. If she is neglectful of her everyday duties or negative about the problems that life brings her way, her attitudes will be reflected in the thoughts and actions of her husband and children.

Women have a position in the family that is like no other. God has created a role that can only be filled by the emotions, discernment, and compassion of the woman. This does not undermine the importance of the man. He is equally important to God's perfect design for the family. The man is the head, the protector, and the provider. God often gives the man insights and wisdom that only he can see.

Ah, but the woman. Here is a creature that possesses almost supernatural abilities. Take her radar sensor, for example. She can detect a troubled situation at the other end of the house while talking on the phone and loading the laundry into the washing machine at the same time. She knows when the children are "too quiet," and she can spot unbrushed teeth from a mile away. Old Saint Nick can't hold a candle to her. She knows if you are sleeping. She knows when you're awake. She's knows if you've been bad or good . . . oh, sorry. I do get carried away sometimes.

Funny thing, the way women work. It's no wonder that men can't understand us. We have powers that they can't even comprehend. Bless their hearts.

My husband and I were having dinner with friends. They were excited as they shared about the arrival of their latest addition, their fourth child. I couldn't help but notice that Jenny, the mom, looked exhausted. I inquired about the baby's sleeping pattern at night.

Randy, the proud father, immediately spoke up. "She's been the best baby! She has slept eight hours every night for the past week!"

As I assessed the look on Jenny's face, I considered telling Randy to duck. Luckily for Randy, she quickly regained composure as she politely yet firmly replied, "No, Randy, *you* have slept eight hours every night for the past week!"

What is it that immediately wakes a woman from a heavy slumber when the baby cries, while the man remains fast asleep? How does she know when something is not "quite right"? Why does she get a "feeling" concerning whether or not to give her child permission to go on the camping trip? It's the God-given talents and abilities that make her the only person right for the role of wife and mom.

The woman is the queen of the castle. The king prides himself in providing his family with the finest living quarters he can offer, but it is the soft touch of the queen that makes the house a home. It is she who can take a tiny two-bedroom apartment and make it seem like a royal refuge. It is she who can take a monstrous, seven thousand square-foot mansion and transform it into a cozy, charming chateau of love. It is the gentle demeanor and pleasing smile of the woman that permeates the home with a sense of welcoming calm. In this, her king delights. The fragrance of her joyful presence is a tantalizing aroma that scents the home more sweetly than a fresh-cut bouquet of magnolias.

How does the woman live out this "joyful presence"? She doesn't do it by herself. She depends on Christ to enable her. To delight in who we are is to delight in Christ. We are his creation, his servants, his children. Apart from his work in and through us there is nothing in which to delight.

The Heavenly Homemaker

Some women feel that homemaking is not a glamorous or rewarding job. Yet, Jesus himself is a homemaker. Jesus said, "I am going there [heaven] to prepare a place for you" (John 14:2b). While Jesus is obviously more than a home-maker, Jesus expresses his care for his people by preparing a home for them. Homemaking is a divine occupation exemplified in the life of the divine Savior.

When I first began the task of writing this book I did a great deal of research on heaven. Many make the false assumption that heaven is not an actual physical place but rather a spiritual awareness, devoid of the physical properties that are familiar to us on earth. These people envision themselves in heaven as transparent spirits floating around aimlessly, singing hymns and playing harps. Not so. Jesus is preparing a *place* that will be much like a glorified version of earth. Glorified, in that it will be sinless, perfect, and magnificently beautiful. However, we will enjoy many of the same physical things we enjoy on this earth.

There will be light, fruit, water, and trees (Revelation 22:1–2). There will be animals (Isaiah 65:25). There will be eating and drinking (Luke 22:30) and even feasting (Matthew 8:11). And who will prepare for us these delicious feasts consisting of the best of meats and the finest of wines? The Almighty Lord himself (Isaiah 25:6).

We will enjoy these things more fully in heaven. Nearly every description of heaven refers to the fond familiarities of earth—eating, music, water, fruits, animals, trees, and a city with gates and streets. They will, however, be incredibly enhanced.

In his book, *In Light of Eternity*, Randy Alcorn brilliantly compares our heavenly home with our earthly home:

> The Bible speaks of the new heavens and the new earth—not the *non*heavens and the *non*earth. "New" doesn't mean fundamentally different, but vastly superior. If someone says, "I'm going to give you a new car," you'd get excited. Why? Not because you have no idea what a car is, but because you *do* know. A new car doesn't mean a vehicle without a steering wheel, seats, doors, and tires. If it didn't have those it wouldn't be a car. The new car is a better version of what you already have. Likewise, the new earth will be a far better version of this earth. That's why we can anticipate it.[1]

While our earthly home will never be as magnificent as our heavenly home to come, we can still be motivated to follow the loving example of Jesus and "prepare a place" of joy and peace for those we love most.

Fortunately, God has granted women the privilege of being homemakers. He has entrusted us to manage the affairs of the home. In Proverbs 31:27, Solomon describes a wife of noble character as one who "watches over the affairs of the household and does not eat the bread of idleness." Our position as keepers of the home is key to family fulfillment.

God created you, the woman, with a wonderful uniqueness that enables you to build your home and family in accordance with his perfect plan. To follow his calling and accept your uniqueness is to fulfill your purpose. The purpose I write of is not being a wife, mom, and keeper of the home. It's glorifying Christ as a wife, mom, and keeper of the home. The woman talked about in Proverbs 31 was not godly simply because she got up while it was still dark, honored her husband, demonstrated good stewardship, and spoke with wisdom and faithful instruction. As productive and respected as she was, she was nothing without the atoning grace of God. She delighted in serving and worshiping her Creator in all the mundane duties of life. She knew that God created her as a woman, to be a wife of noble character, a nurturing mom, and a homemaker. She glorified God in her femininity.

The world will try to woo you away from your femininity. The world says women should be sexy, materialistic, and feminists. Don't be led astray by fictional characters such as the glamorous, sexy wife and mom from "Spy Kids" who finds time to keep her home immaculately clean while leading her family in exciting adventures to save the world. It's fun to watch but don't be deceived. Real women don't live like that. Those who take the bait find themselves snared by the stinging hook of discontentment.

God wants us to delight in who we are. He wants us to laugh, smile, and conduct ourselves as women who have it all—because we do. True beauty radiates from a woman who gracefully walks the path designed uniquely for her. To walk the path of God's will is to show others the beauty of Christ.

If you are wondering how on earth you, "just a homemaker," can make a bit of heaven in your home, you need to understand that as the bride of Christ you can learn directly from the Bridegroom himself, as we will explore in the next chapter.

God created you to be his child, your husband's wife, and your children's mother. True contentment comes in knowing and loving who you are—and *whose* you are. Let us celebrate the beauty and fulfillment of being the nurturers and caregivers of our families. Let us glorify Christ as we delight in his plan for our lives. And let us be happy at home.

Two

Being a Beautiful Bride of Christ

*W*HEN YOU LOVE SOMEONE, you desire to spend time with that person. Think back to the time when you were dating your husband. Remember how you longed to be with him? How everything you did and said and thought revolved around him? When he wrote a letter, you delighted in reading it over and over again. Butterflies tickled your tummy each time your mind replayed that first kiss. Then you would rewind the image and play it over and over again, giddy with every flutter of the butterflies' wings. There is nothing like a young woman in love.

While your groom filled your head with sweet dreams and caused your heart to race, he is nothing compared to your Groom to come. When Jesus Christ comes as the bridegroom to claim his bride (his children) it will be the ultimate love rush, like nothing you have ever experienced. The wedding will be spectacular. At that moment, your beauty will come from within and it will shine more lovely than the most elegant wedding gown or delicate veil this world has to offer. John prophesied of the exquisite beauty of "the bride" to come: "It [the bride] shone with the glory of God, its brilliance was like that of a very precious jewel, like jasper, clear as crystal" (Revelation 21:11). You will also take pleasure in an eternal honeymoon that will never grow old. John offers a glimpse: "Now the dwelling of God is with men, and he will live with them. They will be his people and God himself will be with them and be their God. He will wipe every tear from their eyes. There will be no more death or mourning or crying or pain, for the old order of things has passed away" (Revelation 21:3–4). Now that's what I call a honeymoon!

Perhaps you do not see yourself as the glorious bride that Christ adores. You may think, "God could never want me because he knows about the things I've done in the past. He knows the things I secretly struggle with now." Yet God sees us very differently than we see ourselves. If you have accepted Jesus as your Lord and Savior, God sees you clothed in the righteousness of his Son. He sees you holy and pure, cleansed and blameless—a bride to adore!

God talks a lot about you in the Bible. He calls you his elect, his chosen, his own daughter, a divine masterpiece, a work of art, and a sweet perfume. He says you are fearfully and wonderfully made, forgiven, and precious. He adores you and longs to be with you. You are without fault in the eyes of God. The blood that Jesus shed cleansed you from your sins and made you worthy of being his bride. Rather than a wedding gown, he has covered you in a glowing white robe of his own righteousness.

He waits at the end of the aisle anticipating your arrival. He beckons you to walk the aisle and come before the throne of Holiness to stand with him, the Son of God. Popular tradition has the bride and groom separated on their wedding day until the moment of the actual ceremony. Unlike popular tradition, you can be with Jesus now as you wait for the moment of celebration, the day you can worship and praise the King of Kings in person.

Unlike our wedding ceremonies today, where the focus is more on the bride, the focus of our uniting with Christ will be on the Bridegroom. Although the uniting will be more fulfilling than anything we have ever experienced, the ceremony is not for our pleasure, but his. We are presented to him as living sacrifices, holy and pleasing. It will be a spiritual act of worship and we will not want the glory. We will fully grasp the fact that none of it was ever about us, but about him. I can't wait to be where I don't struggle with making everything about me. I long to worship him completely, without my sinfulness getting in the way. What a day of rejoicing that will be! Our cups shall run over with love as we fix our eyes on Jesus and give him the glory forever and ever!

You are the bride of Christ. Developing your love relationship with him enables you to reproduce a bit of heaven in your earthly home.

Letting Love Flourish

Love is all about priorities. Our top priority is clearly stated in Scripture. It is to love God (Mark 12:30). Our love for God is developed and strengthened through the devotion of time spent together. Fellowshiping with God on a regular basis may seem overwhelming to some women. Perhaps you have never spent time with Jesus and you don't know where to start. Start by listening. The Bible was written for you. It's your huge love letter from the Almighty Lord, that you might know him better.

Whether you already have a relationship with Jesus, but just have trouble being consistent in spending time with him, or you have never really developed a relationship with him and would like to begin that now, here are a few tips:

Focus on Christ, not yourself. We recently had a guest preacher at our church who began his sermon by reading the entire first chapter of Genesis. As he went through the days of creation, I thought, "This is nice . . . a little review never hurt anyone." However, somewhere between "Let the water under the sky be gathered to one place" and "Let the land produce vegetation" my mind drifted to the roast baking in the oven at home. I tuned back in around verse 27: "So God created man in his own image." Why did I lose interest in all the verses in between? Because they weren't about me! We tend to enjoy reading and memorizing Scriptures that pertain to "us." Often, we leave out the second half of a verse because it doesn't grab us like the first part. For example, the first part of Psalm 46:10 says, "Be still and know that I am God." We acknowledge this Scripture because it applies to *us* and *our* needs. It's comforting to "be still before the Lord," especially in the midst of trials and suffering. Can you recall the second half of that verse? I couldn't. The second half says, "I will be exalted among the nations, I will be exalted in the earth." It applies to God's glory, not to us. The blessing we receive of resting in the Lord is secondary to the glory it brings God when we obey.

How about the second half of Ephesians 2:6–7? The first part says, "And God raised us up in Christ and seated us with him in the heavenly realms in Jesus Christ . . ." Sounds nice. I like the idea of being raised up to sit beside God in the heavenly realms. The second part tells *why* we will be raised up: ". . . in order that in the coming ages he might show the incomparable riches of his grace, expressed in his kindness to us in Christ Jesus." The fact that we are raised up is only the means that accomplishes the greater purpose of revealing God's power and grace. We mustn't focus on the means, but the purpose, which is to glorify God in all things.

Even salvation is not solely for our own sake. Christ didn't die on the cross just so that we could avoid hell, or so that we could live blessed lives. Christ died on the cross to glorify his Father. Our salvation is secondary. As Jesus faced an agonizing death, his heart was troubled. He said, "Now my heart is troubled and what shall I say? 'Father save me from this hour?' No, it was for this very reason that I came to this hour" (John 12:27). Before I continue with the next verse, I'd like for you to ponder what it does not say. It does not go on to say that the reason for Christ's death on the cross was for the salvation of mankind. Instead, Jesus surrendered to a painful death as he focused his attention on his Father's will: "Father, glorify your name!" In his prayer recorded in John 17:4, Jesus said, "I have brought you glory on earth by completing the work you gave me to do." Jesus died on the cross primarily for the glory of his Father. He died that our salvation would make the grace and mercy of God known to all generations. It's not about us; it's about God.

Begin with small goals. Pick up a little devotional book or Bible study at your local Christian bookstore to help organize your Bible reading. Jot down things you would like to pray about in a notebook or journal and spend a few minutes talking to God each day.

Have your devotion at a time when you will not be interrupted. Jesus gives us an example of choosing a good time from his own life. "Very early in the morning, while it was still dark, Jesus got up, left his house and went off to a solitary place, where he prayed" (Mark 1:35). Because it was still dark, he probably met with the Father before any of his disciples were awake. I know it's almost impossible for me to spend quality time with Jesus while others are up, whether it's my children, the phone, the doorbell, or even the temptation to see who is online.

Also, when we rise early in the morning to worship and praise our God, we are preparing ourselves spiritually for what the day will bring. "In the morning, O Lord, you hear my voice; in the morning I lay my requests before you and wait in expectation" (Psalm 5:3). While I do enjoy and benefit from having my "quiet time" with God in the mornings, I struggle with falling asleep. If you, too, have this problem, I encourage you to shower first. Make some coffee. Jog around the block if you have to. Do whatever it takes to wake up so that you will be alert to what God has to say.

You might maximize your time with God by praying, repeating Scripture, or singing praise songs while you are showering, exercising, or preparing breakfast. This allows more time to feast on God's Word before your children wake up or other duties call for your attention. However, you must find what works best for you. My friend, Lisa, feels closer to God by "journaling" her prayers, so she allows enough time to write in the mornings.

Be flexible if you have a baby. Please know that you do not have to have your quiet time in the morning. If you have a baby that is still waking for nighttime feedings, you need to sleep while your baby sleeps. Don't be discouraged with this season of your life. Just learn to use your time wisely. If you can't have a sit-down devotion at the same time every day, it's okay. God knows the desires of your heart and he knows what season of life you are in. In fact, he orchestrated the season of life you are in.

Be creative. You could take your Bible with you to appointments and utilize that time in the waiting room. You could place all the Bibles you own in different rooms of the house. Have them opened so that you can snack on God's Word throughout the day as you move from room to room. A little snacking can prevent starvation as you wait for opportunities to feast.

Having a baby can sometimes keep you homebound, where you are unable to attend functions that encourage your growth as a Christian. Consider having an accountability partner. Perhaps another homebound mom who can ask, "What is Jesus teaching you today?"

Also, listening to biblical teaching on Christian radio helps a stay-at-home mom receive instruction, especially if she can't always be at church or attend a regular Bible study.

Be in constant fellowship with God. No one should have a structured time with God each day and then check him off the list. In 1 Thessalonians 5:17 we are told to "pray continually." Remember that prayers do not have to be elaborate or lengthy. Jesus condemned this sort of praying in Matthew 6:7–8 when he said, "And when you pray, do not keep babbling like pagans, for they think they will be heard because of their many words. Do not be like them, for your

Father knows what you need before you ask him." Jesus prefers us to come to him with the simple faith of a child. He said, "I tell you the truth, unless you change and become like little children, you will never enter the kingdom of heaven" (Matthew 18:3).

God wants to hear from you anytime and anywhere. If Aunt Ruby's battle with cancer comes to mind while you are making a bed you might say, "Please comfort Aunt Ruby today, Lord." If Vacation Bible School comes to mind while you are picking up toys you might say, "Lord, let the children who don't know you respond to your prompting." If a sin which you have committed comes to mind while you are washing dishes, don't delay. Pray while you rinse. God will meet you where you are.

My brother was deeply convicted to pray continually by Mrs. Ilze West, a godly prayer warrior in our church. He was riding in the car with her when they witnessed a motorcycle wreck. The driver lost control of the bike while traveling at approximately 45 miles per hour. The bike fell over on its side and slid across the pavement at least 20 yards. My brother, Steven, recalls how Mrs. Ilze's prayer shot out of her mouth like a lightning bolt. "Help him, Jesus!" was voiced before the bike even hit the pavement to begin its sideways skid. Steven describes her "prayer draw" as being faster than any Clint Eastwood cowboy showdown he had ever seen. Now that is a woman in tune with God!

Attend church regularly. Attending church is another way to know the Lord better. Paul tells us in 1 Corinthians 12, that God has called certain men to preach. If God has called certain men to preach then he has something to say through those men. I want to hear everything Jesus wants to tell me.

Also, fellowshiping with other believers encourages you spiritually. God created us as social beings and he knew that we needed to meet together. His instructions are clear, "And let us consider how we may spur one another on toward love and good deeds. Let us not give up meeting together, as some are in the habit of doing, but let us encourage one another—and all the more as you see the Day approaching" (Hebrews 10:24–25).

Meeting together as a team of believers is like cheering at a pep rally before the anticipated Super Bowl, only better. We already know who wins. Church is the only pep rally where you can celebrate the victory before the finale even begins. Let us meet together and rejoice in the approaching Day!

Focus on Christ, not yourself. Let me finish this list by reminding you of the first—and most important—item I mentioned. Satan would have us focus on what God has for us rather than who God is. We read, "Delight yourself in the Lord and he will give you the desires of your heart" (Psalm 37:4) and we assume that the gospel is for our pleasure. We read, "Ask and it will be given to you" (Matthew 7:7a), and we conclude that prayer is the lamp we rub in order for the great Genie to grant our wishes and make us happy. God does desire to bless us. The Scriptures tell us that Jesus does delight in answering our prayers: "And I will do whatever you ask in my name . . ." (John 14:13a). But let us stop right there for a moment and, once again, ponder what the last part does not say. Jesus does not go on to say, "So that you will get what you want and be more fulfilled." Instead, Jesus emphasizes the heart of the gospel, ". . . so that the Son may bring glory to the Father" (John 14:13b). Again, it's not about us; it's about God.

Three

Being a Great Wife

OUR HUSBAND NEEDS YOU to make his home a place of peace and rest. Whether he works to bring home a doctor's salary or a fry cook's pay, he is providing for his family by the sweat of his brow. A wife can show appreciation by making his home a haven. No husband wants to come home from a hard day's work to piles of laundry on the bed, a stressed-out fuzzy-slippered wife with no make-up and unwashed hair, dirty dishes hiding the countertop he paid for, whiney kids who are complaining of boredom, and nothing in the oven for dinner. This kind of disorder and chaos wears a man down.

His home should be a refuge, a place he longs for all day. The thought of home should bring visions of a delicious pot roast to satisfy his hunger, a warm bed with freshly washed sheets to rest his body, delightful children that respect his authority, clean and well-organized rooms, and a loving wife.

It doesn't take a wonder woman to create this inviting atmosphere for her husband. It doesn't require your perfect performance. It does take a willing woman who has her priorities in order. This is important enough to repeat: It's about keeping priorities in order. When her priorities are in order, a wife will have a heart to serve her family; along with that desire, she will trust Christ to bless her both when she succeeds and when she fails.

Establishing your home as a haven for your husband is not about being "his slave." What feminists fail to realize is what a joy the husband is to a wife who fulfills his needs. Although our motives should not be selfish, we are blessed when we demonstrate love for our husbands by joyfully meeting his needs. Here are a few ideas to get you started:

Take care of the affairs of the home. I once knew of a man whose wife called him at work on a daily basis, complaining about the goings on at home. "The kids are fighting and driving me crazy. What should I do with them? The washing machine is on the blink again. Will you call the repairman? Can we go out for dinner tonight? I haven't had time to grocery shop. I'm going stark raving mad cooped up in this house with these kids all day. Can you get off early? I have got to get out of here for a while." I watched this dear man wither like a sun-baked tomato as his wife unloaded her duties onto him.

A wife of noble character takes care of the home (Proverbs 31:27). She doesn't put her responsibilities onto her husband. She proves herself capable, and her husband takes pleasure in putting his confidence in her abilities. She is frugal in spending the money he earns, and he trusts her completely. Her husband lacks nothing and does not suffer as a result of her poor spending. "Her husband has full confidence in her and lacks nothing of value" (Proverbs 31:11). A wife who diligently manages the home and faithfully budgets the finances brings comfort and peace to her husband.

Prepare for his arrival. Take time to prepare yourself and your home for your husband's arrival. My children sometimes ask, "Mom, why are you putting on more make-up when we are not going out?" They giggle when I say, "Because I want to look pretty when Daddy gets home." Nothing builds security in the heart of a child more than the assurance that Mom and Dad love each other. My seven-year-old daughter now has her own tube of lipstick just to look nice for her daddy. Remember, little eyes are watching and learning. Little attitudes are being molded into the wife and mom to come.

Give him time to unwind. The minute your husband walks in the door is not the time to bombard him with questions or concerns. Allow him time to rest his mind and body before you approach him with heavy topics. He will be much more attentive to your needs and concerns and offer better input if he has had time to unwind. His mind has been on work-related issues all day. Give him a little while to change gears from work and focus his attention on his family.

Learn how he communicates. Some men are not multi-task oriented. Perhaps you can think about and discuss several issues at one time, going back and forth without missing a beat, while your man likes to focus on one thing at a time. Understanding this difference will save you much heartache. In her book, *Capture His Heart*, Lysa Terkeurst recounts a conversation with her husband, Art, to demonstrate the differences in the thinking patterns of men and women. I laughed and laughed as I read their dialogue:

Lysa: Hi, honey, how was your day?
Art: Good.
Lysa: Mine, too. I took Hope and Ashley for their well checkups today. (Meaning I took the girls to the doctor not because they were sick but because it was time for their annual physicals.)
Art: (Silently wondering what our well water needed to be checked for and how our daughters fit into the same sentence.)
Lysa: (Feeling a little frustrated at his silence, which I interpret as a lack of caring.) And, they were fine . . . (thinking: *Not that you seem to care.*)
Art: (Still wondering what our well water needed to be checked for and how our daughters fit into it.)

Lysa: Anyhow, (obviously annoyed), on the way to the doctor's office, I was driving down Providence Road, and I noticed all the trees had black tape wrapped around them. It appears to be some sort of pest control treatment. Do you think our trees could be in danger of these bugs? Because if so, I think I'd like to try this tape stuff, which is probably a lot safer than spraying chemicals that could harm the children. You know I just don't think our government is doing enough to protect our kids from dangerous pesticides. So, do you think I should spend extra money at the grocery store for organic produce? If so, I'll need you to add some money to my grocery budget.

Art: (Wondering how the well, our daughters, the trees on Providence Road, and the government's stand on pesticides could end in a request to spend more money. He decides to play it safe.) I don't know, honey; I'll have to think about it.

Lysa: (Astonished at his lack of concern for our family's health, begins to cry.) You'll have to think about what? We are talking about our daughters' lives here and all you can say is you'll think about it!

Art: (Baffled, still not understanding how any of this relates to our daughters' lives but clearly understanding I'm asking for more money again.) Why are you so emotional, and why are you always nagging me for more money? (He realizes he shouldn't have said *nagging,* remembering he got something thrown at him the last time he used that word. He regrets his choice of words and ducks just in case.)

Lysa: Nagging? You call caring for our children, *nagging?* You are so insensitive . . . you're impossible. You're not worth wasting any more of my breath! (Stomp, stomp, stomp, slam.)

Art: *Women! What's the deal? And what did she ever say was wrong with our well?*[1]

Lesson learned. When talking to your man, focus on one topic at a time. It's really a healthier way to communicate anyway. You can conversation hop with your girlfriends but give the hubby a brain break and learn to communicate his way!

Little Things Mean A Lot

You do not have to keep the house immaculately clean, prepare a gourmet meal every night, or purchase expensive gifts to show your love for your husband. A little effort can go a long way. I try to do simple things that make home special for him. I like to have scented candles burning in the kitchen and our bedroom. I usually turn our bed sheets down in the evening. Every once in a while, I'll place a fresh cut flower on his pillow. He may find a note on a lunch plate I prepared for him to enjoy at work. Once he came home and found the yard work (his job) already finished. Often he comes home to find the trashcan has already been taken out to the curb (his job). These small efforts say, "I love you, and I want to make home a haven for your enjoyment."

I realized just how much the "little things" mean when I surveyed one hundred husbands with the question, "Name something your wife does (or you wish she would do) that warms your heart and makes you feel loved?" Based on the many marriage books I've read which harp on the importance of fulfilling his sexual needs, I expected "sex" to be the number one answer to this question. Much to my surprise, it was not. Most of the husbands said it was the small acts of kindness that meant the most to them. Seventy-two percent said that words of encouragement, words of appreciation, and encouraging notes make them feel loved. Mitchell of Auburn, Alabama, articulated this view well:

"Our wedding song was entitled, 'Always.' It was the perfect song to represent our commitment to always love one another, no matter what. She leaves me notes that simply say 'always' in surprise places, such as my sock drawer, my toolbox, under my pillow, in the shower, etc. Sometimes she unrolls the toilet tissue, writes 'always' and rolls it back up for me to find. One day, I opened the garage door and found a huge 'always' banner stretched across the wall! She doesn't have to cook a gourmet meal or buy elaborate gifts. It's the little things that mean a lot."

In addition to words and notes of encouragement and appreciation, husbands also expressed how much it means to have the "support" of their wives. Forty-one-year-old Scott said it best:

"She supports me and believes in me, even when she disagrees."

Another surprising response from these husbands who were surveyed was the importance they placed on the "attitude" of their wives. In fact, thirty percent mentioned how they like to see their wives' smile. Eric, a software programmer, expressed it this way:

"A warm, caring smile does wonders. To think that I had anything to do with that truly lifts me up."

While I had these husbands sharing their hearts, I also asked each one (including my own!) to define his idea of a peaceful home. Once again, the answers were not what I expected. I've always thought that it was the woman who thrives on "talking things through" while the husbands would rather "wait it out." Not so. Over half the respondents said that a peaceful home is a place where conflict is resolved calmly and with an unselfish consideration for the other person. The following anonymous response summarizes this view:

"A peaceful home is not necessarily quiet, but it's loving—even when family members are at odds."

The second most popular definition of a peaceful home was, "a home that serves as a refuge from the outside world." Husbands shared how comforting it is to enter a pleasant, calm, and welcoming haven where they can shut out the rest of the world.

Many husbands shared specific "little things" that make them feel loved:

"She wakes up every morning to kiss me even though I leave the house before 5:00 a.m. Also, she sits on the couch, grabs a cushion, and asks me to let her rub my feet almost every night. She says it's so she can relax."—R.P.

"It means a lot when my wife gets up early with me and makes coffee, even though she doesn't drink it."—J.C.

"When I am tired, she rents a good movie, pops popcorn, and snuggles with me on the couch."—V.B.

"I feel loved because my wife makes me a priority in her life, whether it's going out and getting something she knows I need, or readjusting her schedule to accommodate mine."—A.P.

"She does little things that she knows I like, such as making flavored coffee for me or surprising me with little gifts."—J.F.

"She kisses me when I get up, when I go to bed, when I leave, and when I come home from work."—P.W.

"She cooks special meals just for me."—D.A.

Study your husband and know what makes home special for him. In order to know what your husband likes and dislikes about his home ask yourself: What things does he notice and make positive comments about? What things does he complain about? Better yet, ask *him* what would make his home life more fulfilling.

Once you know *what* to do, the battle is won, right? Sorry—wrong! I know it's not that easy. We all have days when our best intentions give way to survival strategies. Perhaps the dog eats that delicious pot roast while you are re-washing the clean laundry that caught the mug of coffee you set down to answer the phone call about unexpected visitors, right before you discovered your two-year-old had a fever. How do you keep your focus on making your home a haven when you need a haven too?

You absolutely can't do it in your own strength. You can never be strong enough, smart enough, resourceful enough. Putting others first just doesn't come naturally. Laying aside what you want, to serve another with grace and contentment—that is what God calls you to. You can do it only when you rely on the strength that Christ works in you, the love that he supplies, and the perseverance that the Holy Spirit provides.

Our husbands need us to support their decisions, speak words of encouragement, show appreciation for what they do, and respect them as the head of the home. They need a place of refuge where they can relax and wrap themselves in the love of their family. As loving wives, by God's grace, we can prepare that place!

Four

Being a Great Mom

SEVERAL YEARS AGO I found myself at my wits' end. I had changed one too many diapers, cleaned one too many messes, and refereed one too many arguments over "who got to the kitchen table first." I mean, who cares who got to the kitchen table first? It's not like I'm going to refuse food to the one who came in second. Wait. I'm getting off the point here. See? This happened years ago and just rehashing it causes me to resort to a five-year-old's line of thinking. <clearing throat> What I would like to focus on is the revelation I received from God that day. I wrote about it in my book, *Don't Make Me Count to Three!*

If I have to answer one more insignificant question, wipe one more runny nose, or bandage one more boo-boo today, I'm going to pull my hair out . . . and maybe the hair of whoever is standing close by also! "I've had it, kids! I'm going to soak in a hot bubble bath and I would strongly advise against any interruptions. Unless someone is dead or dying, do not knock on this door!"

As I ease down into my vanilla-scented bubbles, I pray, "God, is this really what I'm supposed to be doing? I mean, don't you have something really important for me that requires a little more skill than tying shoes and cutting the crust off sandwiches?"

Let me back up and tell you about myself before I reached this point in my life. I wasn't always bordering on the brink of insanity. It wasn't too awfully long ago that I really had it all together. I successfully managed a booming and well-respected business, counseled others in organizational skills, and drove a pretty cool automobile that would NOT seat an entire soccer team, and me, comfortably. I enjoyed television shows that were not hosted by singing vegetables or a purple dinosaur. I never found the milk in the pantry and I never experienced the sheer panic of trying to remember whom I was calling before the voice at the other end said, "Hello?" Yesterday, I placed an order by phone. When the sales lady asked me for my address, I had to put her on hold. I absolutely could not recall my own address. It did finally come to me as I was reaching for the phone book to look it up.

What happened? The stick turned blue. I have traded in Victoria's Secret™ for the stretchy comfort of Hanes Her Way™. I have boxed up my contemporary Christian music and now you'll find me rockin' to "Silly Songs with Larry." Yep, it's good-bye "20/20" and hello Elmo.

Sometimes I think that just getting dressed and making it through the day is all I ever accomplish. "Isn't there something more that you wanted me to do today, Lord?" Finally, I hear that still, small voice. I may not have found a cure for cancer or conquered world hunger, but as I soak in my tub, God gently reminds me of what I did accomplish today. I had the privilege of listening to the hopes and dreams of a handsome young man who thinks I'm the greatest woman in the world. He stands just over three feet tall and only gets really excited over Legos and pizza, but he is funny, charming, and never boring.

I also got to see a bright and precious smile illuminate the sweet face of my five-year-old daughter as I took time-out to invade Barbie's house with green aliens. As she squealed with delight, my heart melted.

I did have a few minutes of well-appreciated privacy, as I was able to sit on the potty without someone banging on the door. I actually jotted this rare event down in my journal under "miracles." I got to read a couple of great classics. Out loud. Move over Dickens, we have moved on to the works of Dr. Seuss. I was also able to dust, organize, clean, counsel, and cook. I kissed away the boo-boos and washed away the tears. I praised, rebuked, encouraged, hugged, and tested my patience, all before noon.

Yes, my greatest accomplishment today was nurturing the two precious children that God has entrusted to my care.

Now let's talk about my greatest challenge today . . . and every day. It is raising these two precious children in the ways of the Lord. God does have an important job for me and it does require much skill. It is my calling, my priority, my struggle, and my goal. I will rise to the occasion and accept the task at hand. I will love, nurture and train my children the way that God has called me to do.

Moms, we need to be reminded of the awesome responsibility God has given us. When we respond to the high calling of motherhood with passion, the rewards are far greater than any we could ever gain outside of that calling. The joys of motherhood are rare and beautiful treasures that can be easily missed if we don't seize the opportunity to grab them.

Being a mom is more than being cook, chauffeur, maid, counselor, doctor, referee, and disciplinarian (to name just a few). It's molding character, building confidence, nurturing, training, and guiding. There is no calling as consuming, challenging, and rewarding. And there is no calling as worthy of our efforts as the *high calling of motherhood*.[1]

Great Moms Point Their Children to Christ

Our goal in developing healthy communication with our children is to point them to Christ. When we talk to them about things that are important to them, we open the door to their hearts. When our everyday talk relates to their world, we have opportunities to discuss God and his involvement in their lives. However, if we only seek meaningful conversation with our children when there is a lesson to be taught, they will not be as attentive during discussions about God's wisdom and truth.

Talking about Jesus should be a natural part of everyday conversation with your children. Model your own relationship with Jesus and how the gospel of truth changes you from the inside out. Tell them when you have fallen short of the glory of God and how thankful you are for the grace, forgiveness, and redemption of Christ. Talk about God answering your prayers, something fresh he is revealing through his Word, and how he is shaping you to be more like him. Let them know how you struggle with sin, but how you are washed in the blood of Christ and clothed in his righteousness. Let them witness how the hope of the gospel motivates you to cling to Christ.

If in your anger you have sinned against someone, tell your child about it. In their presence, acknowledge your need for Christ. Allow them to witness how the transforming power of the gospel leads you to repentance and obedience to God. Ask them to pray with you as you confess, and take them with you as you seek forgiveness from the person you have wronged. When we allow our children to look into our hearts, they are more likely to let us peek into theirs.

Our children need to know that we are on their side. We are not here to rob them of joy, but to point them to the giver of joy. Be cheerful and kind to your children in all situations, whether at play or during times of training and instruction. We are here to encourage them in wisdom and to lead them to freedom in Christ. We are here to point them to the redemption and hope of Jesus. It's not about climbing on a religious soapbox when our children have done wrong. It's about teaching them that all of life, the choices we make, the paths we take, are all about our relationship with Christ. Everything is a spiritual issue. We were created to worship God. Our main purpose in life is to glorify God in everything. Therefore, all that we do is either glorifying him or not. This is the mindset we want to instill.

Great Moms Ask Great Questions

Creating a mindset in a child requires regular, in-depth communication. You need to understand how your child thinks about all kinds of issues. Your job is to show him how his world, and all his issues, fit into God's world. How do you do that?

One way to be a great mom is to find out your child's perspective on the makings of a heavenly home. Once, when we were on the way home from a family vacation, we were all discussing how good it would feel to be back home. I remember asking my son, Wesley (nine at the time), "What warms your heart when you think of home?" I learned something new about him that day. He thought for a moment, then answered, "I love it when you have candles burning on the kitchen table during supper." "Really?" I replied. "I didn't know you liked candles so much." "Yes, ma'am," he smiled, "they make me feel good inside."

The next week, I received an enthusiastic hug after Wesley entered his room to find a scented candle burning on his nightstand. Quite often, love can be shown in providing simple pleasures. Find out what warms the heart of your child and makes home special for him. Then offer those things as a gesture of love.

Communicating is the only way to really know your child. I'm not talking about a one-sided conversation where you instruct and they nod. I'm talking about learning to listen intently to their hopes, fears, dreams, and concerns. Of course, in order for you to listen, they have to talk. Some kids clam up at Mom's attempt to converse. When Mom asks a question, they offer the shortest answer possible. "How was your day at school?" Mom asks. "Fine," comes the barely audible reply. "Are you enjoying your new teacher?" Mom inquires. "Yeah," the child mumbles as he heads for his room.

Study your child and know how to get him to share his thoughts and feelings with you. You can start by learning how to ask the right kinds of questions and being enthusiastically responsive to his answers. Show him you are really interested in what he thinks. In his book, *Now We're Talking! Questions That Bring You Closer to Your Kids,* Robert C. Crosby notes, "Questions are one of the most effective yet perhaps the most underused tools in a parent's toolbox today. Just five minutes in expressing interest in your child will do more to build your relationship with him or her than five months of trying to get him or her interested in you."[2]

Avoid shallow questions that can be answered with a nod of the head or a single word. Rather than asking, "How was your day at school?" you might ask, "What was the best thing that happened at school today?" followed by, "What was the worst thing?" He knows you care and are really interested in his life when you are willing to stop what you are doing and give him your full attention.

Don't use every conversation as an opportunity to counsel and instruct. If every conversation winds up being a lecture, he will soon learn to keep his mouth shut. He will avoid sharing the details of his life with you. Who wants to constantly be told what they can do better? There's no fun in that. But everyone appreciates a listening ear and a caring attitude.

After one of my daughter Alex's gymnastics meets, we discussed the events in detail during the drive home.

"Did you see that instructor on the mat beside you do all those back handsprings in a row? I thought that was incredible!" I commented.

"Did you see Amanda break in line when it was supposed to be my turn on the balance beam? She does that all the time, and it really makes me mad!"

"Yeah, I saw that. I was proud of you for not losing your temper. It would have been hard for me to overlook it the way you did. You were great on the uneven bars. Which is your favorite between the bars and the balance beam?"

Being eager to participate in conversations that interest your child will build an unbreakable bond of respect, excitement, and closeness in the relationship.

In her book, *Being a Great Mom, Raising Great Kids*, author Sharon Jaynes offers fun questions for getting a meaningful conversation started with your child. For example:

1. What do you think heaven looks like?
2. What does Dad do at work?
3. Who do you see as the most Christ-like among everyone you know?
4. If you were going to spend one year on a desert island and could only take three things, what would they be?
5. When was a time I hurt your feelings?
6. When was a time you were really mad at me?
7. If you could be in a movie, which character would you be? Would you be a character who's already in the movie, or would you be someone else?
8. What's the hardest part about being _____(fill in your child's age)?
9. What's your favorite childhood memory?
10. What person in history would you like to visit?

My friend, Deborah, and her family invented a clever game called "Druthers" to get the family talking and laughing. One person asks, "Would you *druther* be a daisy or an asparagus?" The other person responds with which one and why. Of course, the more outlandish the choices, the more fun the responses can be and the more you can learn about each other. By asking, "Would you *druther* be a sea turtle or a famous painter?" you might find out some surprising things about your child!

When your child is heading in a wrong direction, ask open ended questions that cause him to evaluate his heart and motive. When he is honest about his thoughts and feelings, don't scold him. Help him discern matters of his heart by asking questions such as, "What would really make you happy in this situation? Why would this make you happy? What do you think God thinks about this? What would please God in this situation?" These sorts of questions, along with everyday discussions about the goodness and mercies of God in all things, will weave a greater understanding of the gospel into the hearts of our children. An effort to instill gospel truths, a commitment to prayerful intervention, and an availability to communicate lovingly and patiently are the makings of a great mom.

One of these days, I'll find myself old and gray, reflecting back over my life. I don't want to regret the special moments I missed with my children because I was busy pursuing a career. I want to rock in my porch swing with a wide, perhaps toothless, grin stretched across my wrinkled face as I reminisce of the times my children and I strolled around the block, slid down the fireman's pole from the tree house, laughed over a funny book, threw a Frisbee in the backyard, and roasted marshmallows around a crackling fire. Those are the things that will bring contentment to my heart and assure me of time well spent. Those are the things that will embed precious memories of home into the hearts of my children.

PART TWO

Home is Heavenly

When Unity Prevails

Cultivating Unity in Marriage

WHEN IT COMES TO HAVING A GREAT MARRIAGE, unity is the key. Now, having said that, do you want the good news or the bad news first? Okay . . . the good news. A marriage built on the foundation of unity offers an amazing sense of satisfaction and fulfillment that far exceeds any other human relationship you have ever experienced. Sounds like marriage bliss, huh? Now, the bad news. Unity takes a lot of time and effort.

"A lot of time and effort" is the bad news only because, if you haven't pursued unity in your marriage, it will be difficult at first. However, if you work on unity through the suggestions I am about to make, you will find that "getting there" is half the fun!

When each marriage partner has unity with the other, the unbreakable bond that Christ has with his children is exemplified. Paul explains, "For this reason a man will leave his father and mother and be united to his wife, and the two will become one flesh" (Ephesians 5:31). We are made in the image of God, for the purpose of glorifying God, by our efforts to be like Christ. God uses the marriage relationship to shape and mold us to be more like him. As we strive to be

51

unified through an unselfish effort to meet the needs and desires of one another, we are transformed into his likeness.

Loving the Unlovable

(The Christian husband)

Let's face it. We are all unlovable at times. We have all demonstrated selfishness, greed, envy, lust, rage, slander, evil thoughts and many more indulgences that come from our sinful nature (Matthew 15:19). These are not pretty qualities, but they are bound within our hearts. They will certainly rear their ugly heads, making us not so easy to love at times. Yet, in spite of these moments of weakness and failure, our Heavenly Father views us as perfect. He loves us not in accordance with our nice or naughty ratio, but in accordance with his unconditional mercies and grace, which have been given to us through the life, death, and resurrection of Jesus.

Not only does he forgive us and remember our sins no more, but he clothes us in the righteousness of Christ. When he looks at us, he doesn't see our sins. He sees hearts that have been purified through Christ's work at Calvary. He sees us washed whiter than snow by the redemptive blood of Jesus. He sees us as being perfect.

Since Christ sees me as righteous regardless of my failures, who am I to judge and/or reject my spouse in accordance with his failures? The man I married is justified and accepted by God, so who am I to withhold justification and acceptance? Am I greater than God? Certainly not. I am forgiven, accepted, and transformed, therefore, I will see my husband as forgiven, accepted, and transformed to perfection in Christ.

While I offer practical tips for building unity in this chapter, unity is not acquired simply by following these tips. Unity is acquired through viewing ourselves and others through the lens of the gospel. Unity is not achieved by our own good efforts to get along with our mates by overlooking their offenses or giving up our right to be right. If this were so, we would need nothing more than the law. The law is merely what points us to our need for Christ. When we try to follow God's law and fail, we realize we need help. We cannot keep it apart from Christ. Eventually, we can't overlook the offenses anymore; eventually, we insist on being right. "So the law was put in charge to lead us to Christ that we might be justified by faith" (Galatians 3:24).

When we base our righteousness on keeping the law we become self-reliant and self-righteous. However, when we realize that we cannot truly love and accept others apart from the supernatural indwelling of the Holy Spirit working in and through us, we lay the burden of self-reliance at the cross and embrace the freedom of Christ's righteousness. He already achieved what we cannot.

So remember, unity cannot be achieved by adhering to a list of guidelines. True biblical unity can only be achieved by the following:

Acknowledging our own sinfulness: "I am not perfect. I say and do things that not only hurt others, but also dishonor God."

Acknowledging that forgiveness and transformation come through Christ alone: "Although I do not deserve it, I am forgiven by God's grace and being transformed into his likeness."

Seeing others as being forgiven and accepted by God regardless of their behavior: "Although this man is making me mad, hurting my feelings, or acting like a jerk, he is forgiven, accepted, and adored by Christ."

Seeing others as being perfected in Christ regardless of their behavior: "While this man is certainly not living up to my standards and expectations for a perfect husband, he has been credited the righteousness of Christ and is being transformed into perfection." Your husband will never be sinless, but he stands before God as if he never sinned.

Disharmony will result if you expect him to earn your approval and acceptance through his behavior. Remind yourself, "Regardless of what he has done, this man is perfect in Christ. I can move forward in my relationship with him with hope in the transforming power of Jesus which is at work in him and me." True unity cannot be achieved by attending marriage seminars, following a counselor's instructions, or keeping lists of what to do and what not to do. True unity comes from living by the grace of God. That's the power of the gospel.

Loving the Unlovable

(The non-Christian husband)

The power of the gospel is also at work if you are a Christian married to a non-Christian man. Your reward may not come from your husband, but the Lord will sustain you with his joy and confirmation when you freely give of yourself. It's hard to love someone that seems unlovable, and it's impossible without Christ. It is only by the work of Christ in us that all things become possible. In fact, loving the unlovable can be an awesome opportunity to exemplify Christ in a powerful way.

Christ humbled himself, came to earth, and served. Did he do this for lovable people worthy of his service? No. He did it for sinners. Sure, some loved and appreciated him, but most did not. Yet, the insults, persecution, and hatred hurled upon Jesus did not stop him from pouring out his love, even when it cost him his own life. Jesus not only loved the unlovable, he died for them. By giving of himself completely, he won the love of others.

In the same way, Christ has called wives to serve their husbands, no matter how unworthy they may be. The fact that loving the unlovable is against our nature makes the light of Christ all the more radiant. When we allow his strength to shine through our weakness by loving an ungodly husband, we exemplify a God who loves an ungodly sinner.

"But God demonstrates his own love for us in this: While we were still sinners, Christ died for us" (Romans 5:8). While our husbands are still lost and without the grace of God, we can die to ourselves and by his grace, serve our husbands wholeheartedly. Many men have been won to Christ through the behavior of their wives.

Now, let's consider some of the practical things you must do to nurture your relationship, whether to a Christian or a non-Christian husband.

In order for unity to prevail there must be intentional intimacy. You're probably thinking, "Now hold on a minute! I thought this book was about how to have a peaceful home! Are you *really* going to talk about the 's' word?" In short . . . yep.

Intentional Intimacy

Unfortunately, in today's culture it's hard not to relate the word "sex" with negative or even immoral connotations. Society has given many people (even Christians) a warped view of intimacy. The media has taken something pure and perfect, created to be an absolute pleasure for a husband and wife to share, and turned it into a self-indulgent perversion.

The mere fact that "sex" is constantly talked about in our culture, yet rarely talked about in church, is evidence of the fact that its holiness has been tainted.

A preacher was invited to give a talk at a women's health symposium. His wife inquired about his topic, and he was too embarrassed to admit he had been asked to speak about sex. Thinking quickly, he replied, "I'm talking about sailing."

The next day at the grocery store a young woman who had attended the lecture recognized the minister's wife. "That was certainly an excellent talk your husband gave yesterday," she said. "He really has a unique perspective on the subject." Somewhat chagrined, the minister's wife replied, "Funny you should think so. I mean, he's only done it twice. The first time he threw up, and the second time his hat blew off."[1]

While that is a funny story that makes us chuckle, it is a prime example of viewing sex in the wrong light. The pastor was embarrassed to tell his wife that he was to speak on the subject of sex. Sex is not an aspect of marriage that is embarrassing. It is a holy union that God created for our enjoyment. There is nothing dirty about it, and we certainly shouldn't be ashamed of enjoying one another's bodies within the bonds of marriage.

God had our best interest in mind when he gave us the precious gift of sexual intercourse. He makes his intentions for sex clear in his Word:

Sexual intimacy is for unity. "And the two will become one flesh" (Ephesians 5:31b). When husband and wife come together physically, they become so connected and unified in body, soul, and spirit that God actually sees two separate beings as one.

Sexual intimacy is for giving life. God commands us to "Be fruitful and increase in number . . ." (Genesis 1: 28). How magnificently appropriate for God to bless us with children through his gift of lovemaking!

Sexual intimacy is for pleasure. God desires us to take pleasure in sexual intimacy so much that he had Solomon devote a whole book of the Bible to it. In fact, God has more to say about husbands and wives enjoying sex than he does about "being fruitful" or "being one." Read Song of Solomon and see how God delights in our taking sexual pleasure in our spouses.

Sexual intimacy is for knowledge. "Now Adam knew [had sexual intercourse with] Eve his wife, and she conceived and bore Cain" (Genesis 4:1, NKJV). The Hebrew meaning for "sexual intercourse" is "to know." Through our lovemaking, God empowers us with an intimate knowledge of one another; a mysterious knowledge that is sacred and only to be shared between husband and wife.

Sexual intimacy is for overcoming temptation. In Proverbs 5:15, young men are warned to avoid the temptations of sexual lust and encouraged to "drink water from your own cistern, running water from your own well." As wives, we should keep the river of passion flowing and invite our husbands to drink deeply, lest they be tempted to quench their thirsts elsewhere.

Sexual intimacy is for comfort. Lovemaking relieves tension. When our husbands are stressed from work, facing a difficult situation or depressed, we can offer solace through our bodies. When David and Bathsheba were grieving over the loss of their son, they sought comfort in the union of their bodies. "Then David comforted his wife Bathsheba, and he went to her and lay with her. She gave birth to a son, and they named him Solomon" (2 Samuel 12:24).

In their book, *Intimate Issues*, the authors give the example of how one woman brought comfort to her husband through her body:

> My husband was heaped in a chair, deeply discouraged. A friend had betrayed him. "Honey, take off your shirt and lie on the bed. I've got hot oil and am going to massage the tension out of your muscles." As I rubbed his shoulders and back, I could feel his tension evaporate. I took off his remaining clothes and massaged the rest of his body. Then I comforted him with my love. It wasn't a sensuous time of lovemaking or a glorious time of intimate oneness. It was a time of giving comfort. When he sighed deeply and fell asleep, I felt such joy because of the love I had been able to give.[2]

What a beautiful picture of a wife comforting her husband! For all of these reasons, God gave us the gift of sex. Because sex is part of God's plan for marriage, it is vital that the physical relationship be nurtured. While writing this chapter I began to wonder if the need for sexual fulfillment lessens as couples grow old. I approached my husband's eighty-year-old grandparents with the question, "At what age do couples quit having sex?" As they glanced at each other with smiles of fond familiarity, Mamaw Parker giggled as she replied, "I wouldn't know, Ginger. I reckon you'll have to ask some folks older than us!"

I must admit that I really wasn't surprised by her answer. This is a couple that radiates peace in their relationship. There is peace in enjoying the physical pleasures granted to us from a God who knows our needs.

We often think that our sex lives are lacking if we aren't spontaneously surrendering to fits of passion like they do in the movies. In our married lives we can become so busy that our energy is spent in other places, such as cleaning house, tending to children, and running errands. This is why we must be "intentional" in intimacy. Just because we plan it doesn't mean it's not romantic. In fact, the planning itself tells your mate, "I've been passionately thinking about you today."

Your man needs to know that you want him physically. A pastor's wife once told me that she has never turned down her husband's advances. When I asked her if she always "felt like it," she responded, "Sometimes I don't. However, when I willingly and passionately surrender myself to my husband's desire, God honors my efforts by granting me extra energy . . . and I always wind up enjoying it."

In order for sexual unity to be all it can be, there must be the "foreplay" of time spent talking, laughing, and dreaming together. The best way to accomplish this goal is to plan time alone. Can't afford a babysitter? There are many couples who would love a date night. Consider rotating watching one another's children. In trading nights, you are not only nurturing your own marriage relationship, but you are also enabling another couple to do the same.

Date Your Mate

Don't let the sizzle fizzle. Don't let money keep you from dating. When my husband and I were dating, he was a full-time student who couldn't afford the standard date of dinner and a movie. Our dates consisted of walking hand in hand around the college campus, playing basketball at the city's recreational department, and eating barbeque at my parents' restaurant. I can honestly say that our dates were "richer" than dates I experienced with young men who had money to burn. You don't need mucho bucks to have a meaningful date with your husband.

My husband and I are busy people. With my speaking, writing, and home schooling and his running two restaurants, flying airplanes, and playing with the kids, we need time to focus on our relationship. We are blessed to have parents who place a high priority on spending time with their grandchildren. Once a week, my kids spend the night with my parents. Jim and I have come to cherish our time together. We spend time talking about the past, the present, and the future. We reminisce together. We laugh together. We plan together. We dream together.

Whether you already have an established date night or you are just beginning, avoid the dating rut of ordering pizza and renting a movie. Been there, done that. There's a better way. Believe me, you can have a blast together by making the most of simple ideas for dating. Consider the following ideas:

- Create your own progressive dinner by trying four different restaurants for appetizer, salad, entree, and dessert. To save money, you could split each portion rather than ordering two at each restaurant.
- Re-create your first date. Reminisce about things that were said and the way you felt.

- Walk hand in hand around a lake or along a river or beach. No bodies of water near by? Find a walking trail or even a serene cemetery.
- Be adventurous. Go canoeing or kayaking.
- Go to a flea market or yard sale together and buy one another a gift for under $5.00.
- Take turns planning a creative, surprise date for $10.00.
- Eat dinner by candlelight at home then go out to a nice restaurant for dessert.
- Take some sort of lessons together.

After a few years of marriage, many couples become more like business partners. They make decisions as investors, as home managers, and as caregivers of their children. Yet, they do not take time to bond as husband and wife.

A strong relationship comes from time spent together. Save up and go away for a weekend once or twice a year. Do things you did when you were dating. Tell your man how handsome he is and specific things about him that you like. You will fan a flame of love that will warm both of your hearts in ways you can't even imagine. It's all about giving of yourself, putting him first, being his encourager, and giving your all to please him. We shouldn't give to get, but when you nurture your husband and build him up in all things, you will experience a God-given, rich and satisfying joy.

Letting Your Husband Lead

THE AIR WAS WARM, yet not too warm. The dogwoods were in bloom. The flowers were arrayed in brilliant colors and sweetly scented on this cloudless, blue-skied spring morning. It was the perfect morning to buy a Jeep Wrangler. I woke with a smile. We had discussed it the night before. We had the money, the desire, and the Jeep picked out. Life was sweet. It was a fine day for a Jeep ride.

Jim left for work with a check and a smile. The plan was that he would buy it and come home to pick up the kids and me around 2:00 PM. We would then take a long enjoyable ride in our new toy. Well, two o'clock came and my husband arrived home in his same old boring truck that he had been driving for six years.

With my hands on my hips, I politely, yet firmly asked, "Where's the Jeep?"

Jim simply stated, "I just didn't feel right about getting it." I could see my dreams of cruising around with the wind in my hair and sun on my face being shattered by this man who "just didn't feel right about it." Boy, was I ticked.

"What do you mean you didn't feel right about getting it? If my recollection is correct, you were just as excited about getting it as I was. So, unless you had some revolutionary vision in your sleep last night or heard God's audible voice, I don't think you should change your mind for such a lame reason."

As I stood with eyes a little wider than normal, eyebrows raised, and lips pressed somewhat tightly, I waited for—no, dared—him to offer an explanation.

Calmly he said, "I don't know why. I want you to know that I did pray about the feeling I had. I made it all the way to the car lot with the check in my hand ready to hand it to the guy before I finally surrendered to this feeling. When I walked away I had a peace. You are going to have to trust me on this. We are not getting the Jeep."

This was the first time in our marriage that Jim insisted we were not going to do something regardless of how I felt.

I got over it for a while, but then came our anniversary trip to the beach. We had planned on taking the trip in the new Jeep Wrangler. I was a little disappointed as we cruised along in our old car. Thinking about it more and more as we drove, my gentle and quiet spirit slowly began to transform into a mean, aggressive, sharp-clawed cat. Trying to hide my true motive, I sweetly said, "We could have been in the Jeep."

Jim decided not to retort. He said, "Yes, we could have." Then there was silence.

I crawled into the back seat for a little nap. When I awoke an hour later, I crawled back into the front seat. Before I had a chance to fasten my seat belt—it happened.

We were traveling forty-five or fifty miles per hour when someone turned left just forty feet in front of us. Jim barely had time to even touch the brakes before the crash . . . the air bags . . . the glass . . . the horror. Everything seemed to happen in slow motion, as though I had all the time in the world to think about our lives ending. Amazingly, after everything stopped, we were actually okay. The policemen said the airbag kept me from going through the windshield. Jim and I looked at each other as my words spoken just an hour before rang in our ears, "We could have been in the Jeep!"

The new Jeep that I wanted so badly had no air bags, no protection, not even a roof. Without my seat belt on, I would have been thrown from the Jeep, badly injured, or even killed.

You may not always understand the decisions your husband makes. However, God has placed him as the head of the family. When you submit to his leadership, you can rest assured that you are in God's will. Even when you *reluctantly* submit, you will have the covering and blessing of God's protection. God protects wives who let their husbands lead.

But what about the husband who doesn't want to lead? Many men today are content to step down and surrender to the leadership of women. As a result, many women today are leading their homes and their churches.

One reason men have stepped down is the degrading effect the media has on the masculinity of the man. Everywhere we turn, the man is being beaten down. Women are portrayed as being smarter, wittier, and more well-rounded on almost every television show, while the man plays the weaker, dumber role. Men are often made the butt of the joke while women come out on top.

The enemy [Satan] comes to steal, kill, and destroy (John 10:10). In today's culture, he is after our men. He wants them to think they are not worthy to be leaders. He wants them to think they are inferior to women, and quite frankly, he has done a good job.

Unfortunately, many wives play the devil's advocate by undermining every decision their husbands make. Wives complain that their husbands won't lead, but in many cases, they simply won't let them. I believe men today have thrown up their hands as a result of being shot down from every attempt at leadership, whether the snipers are their wives or the cannons of cultural entertainment.

If we shoot them down in the little decisions why should they think we would respect the bigger decisions they make? If your husband says, "Hey, let's go out for dinner tonight," and you respond, "We can't go out for dinner tonight! It's not in the budget!" what is that saying to your man? It's saying, "Your suggestion is stupid. I am more capable of making financial decisions for our family."

If your husband says, "I've been offered a better job in another state, and I believe we should move" and you respond, "We can't move! All of our friends are here, and the kids would be devastated if they had to change schools!" what is that saying to your husband? It's saying, "I do not trust you to make wise decisions for our family." After so many negative responses, many men will give up.

Another reason why many men do not lead is simply due to personality traits. A man who is phlegmatic (passive) in personality will be content to take the back seat and let his wife do the driving. One husband put it like this, "Leading comes more natural to you [his wife] so why don't we just accept that fact and let you lead?" He felt that there would be less arguing if they both agreed for the wife to lead. However, the Bible clearly states that the husband is to be the head. "For the husband is the head of the wife as Christ is the head of the church, his body, of which he is the Savior" (Ephesians 5:23). The Scripture does not say, "Unless the husband is more comfortable forfeiting his position as leader." When a husband is not a natural leader, couples need to take great measures to purposefully place the husband as head of the home.

Personality traits aside, many men today simply do not want to lead. Some are perfectly satisfied to go with the flow and shuck their responsibility as the leader of the family. Even though many women assume (and even strive for) the leadership role themselves, they long to have their husbands step up to the plate and take control. One woman who has taken the leadership role in her family said, "I've tried whining, begging, and manipulating to get my husband to lead. He just won't do it." What this wife doesn't realize is that in order for a ruler to step up another ruler must first step down. After all, is not a wife who is constantly seeking to force her husband into a leadership role, in fact leading? Another woman said, "I just can't submit to my husband. He isn't a Christian, and he has no interest in being the leader in our family."

Could it be that these women are more concerned with changing their husbands than themselves? "Why do you look at the speck of sawdust in your brother's eye and pay no attention to the plank in your own eye?" (Luke 6:41) We are responsible to conduct ourselves as godly wives regardless of whether or not our husbands lead. The Bible doesn't say, "Wives submit to your husbands unless they do not meet your qualifications as a leader." The Bible does say, "Wives, submit to your husbands as to the Lord" (Ephesians 5:22). In other words, we are to submit to our husbands in the same way that we submit to the Lord. If we are not submitting to the leadership of our husbands then we are not submitting to the leadership of God.

We cannot force our husbands to lead but we can make every effort to respect, honor, and submit to them. There is more to respecting them as leaders than simply honoring their decisions. We must learn to trust God.

We Must Learn to Trust God

Because of a woman's natural bent to nurture and protect, she has a hard time moving out of the way. Our instinct is to stand between pain and those we love, so we have an overwhelming sense to be in control. We think we can prevent mistakes from being made. Relinquishing control to our husbands fills our minds with a fearful torrent of "what ifs." What if I submit to him and he makes the wrong decision? What if our whole family has to suffer the consequences of my husband's poor choices? So we fight for control.

It is vital that we learn to trust God's hand in maturing and sometimes disciplining those we love. It would be better for a husband to suffer the consequences of bouncing a check as a result of not keeping the checkbook balanced than never to gain wisdom in financial stewardship. It would be better for him to fail at any given task as a result of trying than to never be man enough to try because of his wife keeping him down.

Also, the husband who is respected as the head of the family will gain confidence as the protector and provider of the family. The man who is made to feel inadequate by a wife who overrules his authority will become weak and handicapped when it comes to making wise decisions.

Build your man up, trust God to lead him, encourage him in his role as the decision maker. Sure, he may make some poor decisions, but with the support of a wife that looks up to him as the man of the house, he will grow stronger and wiser. Trust God to develop him into the man he was created to be.

Resist the temptation to say, "I told you so" or "That wouldn't have happened if you would have listened to me." If he blows it, he knows it—even if he won't admit it. Even if he does blow it from time to time, so what? You are responsible for you, not your husband. When he makes an unwise decision that you submitted to, you are innocent because you are ultimately under God's authority—and he has called you to submit to your husband.

"But Ginger," you say, "if I don't put my foot down to some of the stupid choices my husband makes, we could lose everything we have. The man is an idiot! Our family is better off when I overrule some of his ridiculous decisions." All that we have is in Christ, not in the material things we think we can't live without. Better to lose everything on earth and gain Christ. Paul says it this way,

> "But whatever was to my profit I now consider loss for the sake of Christ. What is more, I consider everything a loss compared to the surpassing greatness of knowing Christ Jesus my Lord, for whose sake I have lost all things. I consider them rubbish, that I may gain Christ and be found in him, not having a righteousness of my own that

comes from the law, but that which is through faith in Christ—the righteousness that comes from God is by faith" (Philippians 3:7–9).

God is good all the time. He always has your best interest at heart. Even when your husband makes an unwise choice, God is at work for your good: "And we know that in all things God works for the good of those who love him, who have been called according to his purpose" (Romans 8:28). God knew every bad decision your husband would make before either of you were born. The same God who parted the sea is also capable of using the worst of situations for good.

Confidence in Christ is what keeps us from despairing at the possibility of a husband's wrong choice. To stress over a decision with which we do not agree is to put our hope and trust in man rather than God—and then be disappointed. It's to carry a burden we were not intended to bear. When our hope and confidence are in Christ, we unload the weight of anxiety and experience confidence in Jesus. David reminds us, "The Lord is my light and my salvation—whom shall I fear? The Lord is the stronghold of my life—of whom shall I be afraid?" (Psalm 27:1).

Trust God by letting your husband lead and resting in the fact that your security is based on the hope of Christ, not on your husband's choices. Comfort him when he blows it and don't respond with an arrogant attitude of superiority. The beauty of the whole thing is that your love will be demonstrated even more powerfully when you support your husband in his failures as fervently as in his successes.

You may have expected this chapter to offer a list of "things you can do to get your husband to lead." Yet, this chapter is not about changing your husband; it's about your heart. It is possible to want your husband to take control and step up as a manly leader so much that it becomes an idol of your heart. Once again, you are not responsible for your husband. God can use even your husband's lack of motivation in leadership to bring you to a deeper level of contentment.

Another way we can encourage our husbands as leaders is by respecting their boyish need to play. Nothing can strip away a man's dignity and masculinity faster than a wife who nags about his natural desire for adventure. If you really want to be a wife who goes above and beyond the call of duty (and win the heart of your knight in shining armor), enter his world of play.

Entering Your Husband's World

Isn't it funny how the personality traits that first attracted us to our husbands drive us crazy later? Take my husband, Jim, for instance. He has always approached adventure with reckless abandon. The fact that he enjoyed rappelling down steep mountains Australian style (upside down) and making 230-foot bungee jumps sent shivers of excitement and intrigue through my entire body, making him the most irresistible man I had ever met. So I married him.

Thirteen years and two kids later, I was frying pork chops when Jim waltzed into the kitchen with that mischievous *boy-have-I-got-an-idea-now* look on his face. The wild zeal in his eyes told me I needed to brace myself for what was coming next.

"I want to fly airplanes," he grinned. I wanted to cover my ears and chant, "I'm not going to listen to you. I'm not going to listen to you." But instead, I decided to be mature about it.

"Have you lost your mind? Do you think I'm going to offer my blessing and seal my fate as a widow at the age of thirty-four? If you do this, I'm never speaking to you again!" (Stomp, stomp, stomp, slam)

Two days and many prayers later, I boldly proclaimed (with one hand on my pajamaed hip and the other waving my toothbrush in the air), "Okay, if you want to do this it's fine with me. But let's get one thing clear, Buddy. Neither I, nor any of your offspring, will ever get in that airplane with you!"

Three months later, I was climbing into the back of the airplane. Jim kissed my cheek and promised, "You're gonna love it." My excessive fear of heights, however, was screaming otherwise. To make matters worse, Jim's flight instructor announced, "Jim, today we're going to work on your shaky landings."

I leaned forward and lightly tapped the instructor's shoulder. "Excuse me, what did you say? For a second there I thought you said we were going to work on Jim's shaky landings."

The instructor chuckled at my anxiety as Jim began speaking some sort of numeric jargon into the microphone. "Auburn traffic Skyhawk eight-niner-eight-four-seven departing runway three-six." But all I heard was, "Mayday! Mayday! Mayday! We're all going to die!"

With eyes tightly shut and sweat pouring from my otherwise calm demeanor, I assumed crash position. I braced myself by pressing my feet against the back of the front seats and my palms flat on the ceiling of the plane (for when we rolled, of course). I began confessing all of my sins as I begged for God's mercy. I felt the plane lift off the runway. Nothing happened. Ten minutes later, I forced open one eye to see if I had arrived at the pearly gates. Nope, it wasn't the pearly gates, but it was something that took my breath away: A thrilling and fantastic view of God's creation.

An overwhelming sense of peace washed over me. I began to bask in the beauty of it all. I began to see what attracted Jim to flying. The freedom of sailing with the clouds over the earth was like a glorious tour of God's handiwork—and my husband was my tour guide. Pride fluttered in my heart as I glanced at his handsome face etched with wild excitement. In spite of his shaky landings, I was glad to share in his adventure that day.

While boys grow up to become husbands, fathers, workers, supporters, protectors, and providers, there is one thing they never outgrow: Their need to play. In the core of every man's heart lies a deep longing for adventure.

There are two types of wives: Those who encourage their husbands in their adventurous pursuits, and those who strip away their masculinity by nagging, belittling, and complaining about their "wilder" sides. Wilder, not in the sense of activities that are displeasing to the

Lord, but activities that enable him to fulfill his need for boyish play. A good wife will support her husband's need to express his manhood. An *excellent* wife will take it a step further by enthusiastically entering her man's world.

Want to spark the fires of romance in your marriage? Try planning a surprise fishing trip for two. A wife who is willing to hook a worm and reel in a bass will warm the heart and win the affection of her fisherman. Want to enhance communication with your spouse? Try driving the golf cart one afternoon, cheering him on, and learning to keep score. If it's football that floats his boat, try snuggling beside him on the couch with chips and dip and asking him to explain the rules of the game. Nothing says "I love you" more than your willingness to invest time in your husband's hobbies. Here are a few tips for entering your husband's world:

Be understanding. Your husband will be gratified by your support of his God-given desire to conquer, his manly passion for adventure, and his natural tendencies to explore.

Be attentive. A wife who seems indifferent or even annoyed by her husband's adventurous side will dishearten her mate. Stop what you are doing when he returns from play. Give him your full attention and allow him the pleasure of telling you all about it. Share in the things that bring him joy.

Be interested. Genuine interest is best expressed by asking questions. Rather than asking merely, "How was your hunt?" ask for specific details. "Did you see any tracks?" "What was the best part of your hunt this morning?" One wife found that her husband's most intimate times with God happen in the woods. Her sincere inquiries led him to share his deepest spiritual awakenings.

Another way to show interest is to do a little research on his sport or hobby of choice. A little time on the Internet can educate you enough to speak his language. The wife who knows the ins and outs of trying for a two-point conversion or why to avoid stepping inside the key on a foul shot radiates genuine warmth that her man will find irresistible.

Be involved. If at all possible, invest yourself in your husband's interests. Whether he plays basketball, tennis, or chess, offer to participate. If you can't actually do the activity, find a way to get involved. Offering to call and schedule a tee-time for his Saturday golf game or packing snacks along with a sweet note of encouragement for his fishing or hunting trip are simple ways to involve yourself and show support.

Your willingness to be understanding, attentive, interested, and involved in your husband's hobbies sends a powerful message that he is important to you. Embracing his unique qualities and characteristics is to embrace the man that God gave you. Celebrate your husband's adventurous side by showing your support . . . it can open a whole new world in your relationship.

Now that I have offered suggestions for capturing the heart of your man, I have to tell you that you cannot do these things on your own. Sound familiar? I keep repeating this because we forget so easily. We keep thinking we just have to try harder. But to be understanding, attentive, interested, and involved to the extent I am proposing is impossible apart from Christ.

Sure, we can manage an outward effort. But any effort made in our own strength is shallow at best. We are self-centered by nature. We may implement these suggestions, but if we are honest it's often because we want something back. Perhaps we think, "If I show interest and strive to meet his needs, he is more likely to do the same for me." Selfish motives may not be obvious. Or we may think, "If I show interest and strive to meet his needs, he will think I am a wonderful wife." While the latter motive seems to be nobler, both are equal in selfishness. Both are giving to get. Both are manipulative tactics for personal gain.

True love doesn't give to get. It is not self-seeking. We are only able to love by walking in newness of life, which comes from dying to self and living through the power of Christ. As he transforms us into his likeness, his love is fleshed out in action. Therefore, although we cannot love as fully as God commands, we are not without hope. The power of Christ gives us everything we need for life and godliness. We must cling to him who is at work in our lives. Only then can true love come forth.

Entering your husband's world is definitely an adventure. Entering his world with Jesus leading the way promises adventure beyond his (and your) wildest dreams!

Seven

Working Through Conflict Gracefully

JIM AND I ONLY DATED A LITTLE WHILE before we married. In fact, we met and married in eight months. In my eyes Jim could do no wrong. I just knew that we would never argue. After all, who could argue with a perfect man? Much to my surprise, it wasn't long until we found ourselves in the middle of our first argument. This issue was so important that I simply could not back down. I've always been told to "choose your battles wisely," and this was a hill on which I was willing to die. The argument was over . . . sweet tea.

We were fresh from the honeymoon. The aftermath of sheer romance lingered in the air, keeping me light on my feet. All was well, until I decided to make sweet tea. Already having the sugar in the pitcher and the tea brewed, I asked Jim to mix the tea with the sugar and add some water while I went to shower. "Sure," he gladly replied. Two hours later, I came downstairs ready for our night out. I glanced toward the kitchen and saw that the tea had not been mixed with the sugar:

> Ginger: "Sweetie," (I say with a tone that wasn't so sweet) "I asked you to finish making the tea."

Jim: (rushing over to dump the cold tea into the pitcher) "Oh, I forgot. I'll do it right now."

Ginger: (with a look that says "you idiot") "No, it's too late for that now. I'll have to get the water hot again."

Jim: "Why are you looking at me like *I'm* the idiot? Everyone knows sugar dissolves in water. So what if the water's cold?"

Ginger: "Are you calling me an idiot?"

Jim: "No, I'm simply saying that it is a scientific fact that sugar dissolves in water."

Ginger: (still thinking he meant to call me an idiot) "Well, if sugar dissolves in water then why is it that when people order sweet tea at a restaurant and the waiter says they only have unsweetened tea, most people will change their order to something else?"

Jim: (raising his voice) "Because they're idiots. They don't realize that the sole purpose for sugar packets on the table is to sweeten their unsweetened drinks!"

Ginger: "Are you calling me an idiot?"

Jim: (ignoring my question) "Let's just get out a science book and I'll show you that sugar dissolves in water."

Ginger: (walking toward the front door in order to make a dramatic and loud exit after I claim the last word) "No, that's okay! I wouldn't want you to waste your time educating an idiot!"

After driving around for an hour, I returned home to find Jim, my younger brother, Steven, and two pitchers of tea marked "A" and "B" in the kitchen. Determined to settle the issue once and for all, Jim announced, "Steven will now taste the tea from each pitcher and see if there is a difference in cold tea mixed with sugar and hot tea mixed with sugar."

"Whatever," I announced as I headed upstairs.

"What's the matter? You afraid you might be wrong?" Jim asked.

Accepting the challenge, I bounced back down the stairs, lifted my chin and entered the kitchen. Then I glared at my brother, daring him to betray his only sister.

After tasting each one and savoring the fact that his opinion would determine the winner, Steven announced with the voice of a radio broadcaster that he preferred pitcher A. "Uh, Huh!" Jim boasted with his chest sticking out like a rooster. While the boys were high-fiving and strutting around like peacocks, I was screaming, "That is not the point! Who cares which one tastes better! The point is that they are different!"

Needless to say, the "taste test" didn't solve anything because the problem was not whether or not sugar dissolved in cold water. The problem was that Jim and I didn't know how to approach conflict gracefully.

It is important that we remember our ultimate goal in life, which is to glorify Christ in everything, even in the midst of conflict. The book of James says, "Consider it pure joy, my brothers, whenever you face trials of many kinds, because you know that the testing of your faith develops perseverance. Perseverance must finish its work so that you may be mature and complete, not lacking anything" (James 1:2–4). Handling conflict biblically provides opportunity for us to glorify God, serve others, and grow to be more like Christ. Now those are reasons to be thankful!

Want to know the secret to getting through conflict gracefully? It's bleeding Bible when you are pricked. When we keep a Christ-like attitude toward conflict, it will change the way we view it and handle it. Conflict is no fun. It's often painful. But much heartache can be avoided when we are willing to apply God's principles to resolving conflict.

Be willing to overlook minor offenses. "A man's wisdom gives him patience; it is to his glory to overlook an offense" (Proverbs 19:11). Is this really worth arguing over? Is not the relationship more important than being right, especially over a frivolous issue? There are legitimate conflicts worthy of attention, but there is a proper way to approach them. Choose your battles wisely. Give each potential battle the "will it matter" test. "Will this really matter tomorrow; in one year; in ten?" If it's trivial, let it go rather than indulge in verbal combat unnecessarily. "Starting a quarrel is like breaching a dam; so drop the matter before a dispute breaks out" (Proverbs 17:14).

By overlooking inconsequential offenses, we demonstrate the forgiveness of Christ. Thankfully, we serve a God who chooses not to deal harshly with every sin we commit. Exemplify God's goodness by extending grace when you can. This doesn't mean that you use the offense as ammunition later. It means that you cast it away just as our Lord casts our sins "as far as the east is from the west."

Be humble. Pride can be the greatest stumbling block to resolving conflict biblically. To be humble in conflict is to put the needs of another before your own. "Do nothing out of selfish ambition or vain conceit, but in humility consider others better than yourselves. Each of you should look not only to your own interests, but also to the interests of others" (Philippians 2:3–4).

Search your heart and take ownership of your own wrongdoing. Even if you think your spouse is the main culprit, admit your own fault. Be sure to not use the word "but" at the end of your confession, followed by justifications for your sin. Identify what you did wrong by saying, "What I did (name what you did) was wrong," followed by "will you forgive me?"

True humility focuses on one's own wretchedness, rather than the wretchedness of others. Sincere humility can soften the heart of another, bringing a conflict to resolution more quickly. "Be completely humble and gentle, be patient, bearing with one another in love. Make every effort to keep the unity of the Spirit through the bond of peace" (Ephesians 4:2–3).

Be self-controlled. If we speak while angry, we are liable to blurt out words that will inflame rather than extinguish conflict. Sometimes the only way to gain self-control in the heat of the moment is to walk away for a time rather than to poison your relationship with venomous words. As I observed in, *Don't Make Me Count to Three,* "As a small spark can ignite and destroy an entire forest, so can the fiery darts of the tongue destroy those we love most. However, when used properly, the tongue can produce fruit that heals, comforts, and nurtures those we love most."[1]

If you are so angry that you need to walk away, set to praying at once. The Bible instructs us to resolve conflict quickly: "Do not let the sun go down while you are still angry" (Ephesians 4:26). It is vital that you pray, lest the enemy get a foothold and drag things out. If you do not pray, you may be tempted to wallow in self-pity, or worse, bitterness or resentment. It is only when you have gained self-control and can speak in a gentle tone of voice with carefully measured words that you are ready to work toward resolution. Remember, "Reckless words pierce like a sword, but the tongue of the wise brings healing" (Proverbs 12:18).

Be gentle. It's easy to be harsh in the midst of an argument. It's not so easy to act contrary to your feelings by responding gently while your insides are throwing a temper tantrum. Being nice instead of nasty reflects God's power in your life. Guard against speaking harshly, as it will only make matters worse, for "a gentle answer turns away wrath, but a harsh word stirs up anger" (Proverbs 15:1). Salve the wounds of verbal wreckage, rather than inflaming them. A gentle response may encourage your opponent to be gentle too.

Ken Sande tells a story that validates the positive effect a wife can have on her husband if she responds gently, even when he's wrong:

> I recently observed a couple practice this principle in their marriage. The husband had been under a lot of stress recently, and was more irritable than usual. As a result, he was unfairly critical of his wife and said some harsh things to her in my presence. She had every right to confront him for his sin, but God gave her grace to be gentle. Instead of rebuking him, she overlooked her husband's offense, responded with kind words, and acknowledged the difficulties he was facing. After

asking questions to learn more about his situation and feelings, she offered to help him in some concrete ways. He was touched by her gentleness and apologized for the way he had treated her. Thanks to this wife's gentle response, a situation that could have turned into a major quarrel was transformed into a time of real ministry and growth.[2]

Be forgiving. If we embrace God's mercy in our own lives, we can forgive those who have wronged us. Some people get caught up in "rights." "I have my rights. Why should I let him get away with treating me like that?" "Rights" are playing too big a part in our thoughts if they override our duty to biblical morality.

The Bible is filled with examples of mercy, grace, kindness, and forgiveness being extended to the undeserving. Abraham relinquished his right to have the first choice of land in Canaan by allowing his nephew, Lot, to pick his land first (Genesis 13:5–12). Joseph gave up his right to punish his brothers for selling him into slavery (Genesis 50:19–21). In the parable of the unmerciful servant, the master chose not to "exercise his rights" by demanding from his servant the money he owed. Instead, he showed mercy by canceling the debt (Matthew 18: 21–26).

Praise Jesus that he didn't exercise his own right to bring us all to justice. Instead, he gave himself up to death on a cross, thus paying the debt for the very ones that wronged him. Peter explained it like this: "He [Jesus] committed no sin, and no deceit was found in his mouth. When they hurled their insults at him, he did not retaliate; when he suffered, he made no threats. Instead, he entrusted himself to him who judges justly. He himself bore our sins in his body on the tree [cross], so that we might die to sins and live for righteousness; by his wounds you have been healed" (1 Peter 2:22–24). There is no greater mercy, grace, and forgiveness than that which Jesus demonstrates every day on our behalf. Forgive as the Lord forgives you.

Be transformed in your thinking. "Finally brothers, whatever is true, whatever is noble, whatever is right, whatever is lovely, whatever is admirable—if anything is excellent or praiseworthy—think about such things" (Philippians 4:8). It is tempting to dwell on what your husband is doing wrong in the midst of conflict. When you give in to that temptation, your thoughts can then move toward *all* of his bad qualities. Solomon encourages us not to search for the bad, but to seek out the good. "He who seeks good finds good will, but evil comes to him who searches for it" (Proverbs 11:27). Gaining control of your thoughts enables you to focus on the real point of conflict, rather than dragging in unnecessary things that muddy the waters. It enables you to deal honestly and realistically with the issue at hand.

I remember a time when Jim said something that hurt my feelings. I don't remember what it was, but I do remember taking my anger out on the unsuspecting tub. I often clean the house when I am upset or angry. Hmmm . . . now that I think about it . . . could this be my husband's ploy to get me to do housework? Anyway, I set to work, vigorously cleaning the tub while treating myself to a pity party. The Lord interrupted my negative thoughts by reminding me that I was to think about things that are "excellent" and "praiseworthy." "Well, I don't know what's so praiseworthy about what he just said to me!" I prayed in protest.

After several more minutes of pouting, I grudgingly forced myself to think of something good about Jim. He takes out the trash. (You have to start somewhere!) Then, as I opened my mind to receive good thoughts, they slowly began to flood in. Jim is extremely generous. He freely gives of his money and time to others. He's a wonderful dad. He eagerly plays endless games of Clue, Monopoly, and basketball with the kids. He takes me out on a date every week, always asking where I would like to go. He opens my car door for me, no matter how cold it is outside. He works hard to provide for his family. He ministers to others through his restaurant by placing encouraging Scriptures instead of food specials on the marquee.

In light of Jim's many praiseworthy qualities, his comment that upset me suddenly didn't matter. What's one minor flaw in an otherwise great man who blesses me so? I ran out of the bathroom a changed woman. With suds running off my yellow cleaning gloves, I hugged Jim tightly and told him how much I loved and appreciated him. The power of God's Word is an amazing thing.

As you understand God's law of overlooking offenses and being humble, self-controlled, gentle, forgiving, you may become discouraged. You realize that you do not respond in ways that please God and promote peace, and now you are overcome with guilt, regret, and defeat. Remember, if we could obey the Law on our own, there would be no need for the grace and forgiveness of God. Paul reminds, "he saved us, not because of the righteous things we have done, but because of his mercy" (Titus 3:5a).

God convicts, but he also forgives. He not only forgives, he delivers. He not only delivers, he restores. For this reason we are not condemned. Look with hope to a God who forgives, restores, and does more than we can ask or imagine! He gives us his righteousness so that we don't have to despair in our unrighteousness. He has given us everything we need for life and godliness through Christ Jesus. When our eyes are fixed on Jesus, we can look back with peace and look forward with hope. We can hold tightly to Christ who enables us to do every good work. With great confidence we can move forward as ones who are perfected in Christ. What hope there is in the gospel!

Eight

Cultivating Unity Among Siblings

 AM CONSTANTLY REMINDING MY CHILDREN that they are best friends. When they enter an argument, I always say, "You two are best friends." Naturally, siblings are going to argue and get on one another's nerves from time to time, but it's important that parents pro-actively cultivate unity and friendship. Today's culture would like for us to believe that it's normal for siblings to not get along and not "like" each other. This is readily seen in the media. Rarely do movie or television siblings treat one another with respect and affection. They're usually fighting, yelling for the others to "get out of my room," name-calling, or belittling each other with mocking, sarcastic, and even hateful remarks.

This sort of behavior has become *expected*. It's viewed as normal. However, in a Christian home, this should not be so. Jesus commands us to "love one another" and to "put others above ourselves." The sibling relationship is the best place to begin instilling these principles. Brothers and sisters who are trained to treat one another with respect and love will not only enjoy closeness during the growing-up years, but will also delight in a stronger relationship in adulthood. "Practicing" on one another will also prepare them for a healthier marriage relationship. Here are some ways you might move past just being the referee and encourage your children in a well-balanced friendship:

Have a "serving the other" day. Christ didn't come to be served but to serve (Matthew 20:28). Let your children experience the joy of serving by thinking up five ways to serve their sibling(s) one day each month. It could be simple acts of kindness such as making sister's bed, offering to let brother sit in the front seat with mom even though it's not his turn, or doing the other's chores. Make it fun. Let the child who is serving pick his/her own day and try to surprise the sibling with each task. If there are many siblings in the home, you could add to the fun by drawing names and trying to serve without the other finding out who the server is.

Teach them to support one another. I was impressed with my friend, Lena, who wouldn't allow her eight-year-old daughter to come to my daughter's spend-the-night party because her twelve-year-old sister was having a sleepover the same night. Many people might frown on that, using the logic, "Her sister will have all of her older friends over, so why does it matter if little sister isn't there? The sisters probably prefer to be with friends their own age anyway!" Not so with Lena's children. These sisters are growing up as "best friends." This mentality was instilled early on. Therefore, they wouldn't dream of putting other friendships above their own. Their relationship is too cherished for that.

Make it a given that siblings attend one another's special events. If Jimmy is playing his trumpet at a beginner band concert, attendance should not be an option for his brothers and sisters. If Amy is performing at a ballet recital, her siblings should be there to support her with cheers. Prompt your children to encourage and build one another up verbally when they are young and it will become a habit. If they are already older, it's never too late to start. Have a talk with them about developing their friendship and go over the new expectations as a family. There may be some initial complaining, but they will begin to enjoy a stronger, more loving relationship (even if it's forced for a while).

Teach them the priority of their friendship with one another. You shouldn't feel obligated to let them take a friend along on every occasion. Unity is cultivated on outings where siblings enjoy adventures and time together. Always taking a friend can hinder your children from bonding with each other and cause them to become overly dependent on their peers.

I love to have my children's friends over. There are several days each month where we have a whole gang over for pizza, movies, and games. However, I know that it's time to cut back when my children begin to bicker more than normal and treat one another differently. Yesterday, I noticed that my son, Wesley, was belittling almost everything my daughter, Alex, said. We talked through his wrong attitude toward his sister. Then I said, "Alex is your best friend, yet you don't seem to be enjoying her like you do your other friends. Until you can speak to her kindly and treat her with respect, you will lose the privilege of spending time with other friends."

I have pulled the privilege of time with friends several times over the years in order for my children to focus on their own friendship. It always works. They gain a new appreciation for one another as they reevaluate the priority of their relationship. It has never taken more than a couple of weeks of encouraging uninterrupted time together to instill that "best friend" mentality again. It's not punishment. It's not being "grounded." It's pro-actively training them to keep their relationship right.

Pro-actively guide them in settling conflict. If the bickering is really bad, you might have them go in separate rooms (doesn't have to be bedrooms if they share) and not come out until they have done two things:

83

1. Be willing to confess their *own* fault in the argument. This is teaching them to seek forgiveness for their own wrongdoing rather than selfishly dwelling only on the wrongdoing of another. Jesus challenged us: "Why do you look at the speck of sawdust in your brother's eye and pay no attention to the plank in your own eye?" (Matthew 7:3).

2. Write down (or think of) something positive about their sibling and be willing to share it when they come out. This is teaching them to control their thought-life in the midst of conflict by thinking on what is "excellent" and "praiseworthy" rather than stewing over the details of the argument.

Pray that God would give you wisdom as you encourage your children's friendships. Look for ways to encourage them to love one another. When my children were younger, I would prompt them to demonstrate acts of love and kindness to each other. On many occasions I would whisper something like, "Why don't you encourage Wesley by telling him that he did a great job putting his toys away?" or "Why don't you encourage Alex by telling her what a nice job she did coloring her picture?"

Be watchful of attitudes that can damage their friendship, such as jealousy, envy, or distrust. Of all the sinful attitudes that can wreak havoc on sibling friendships, nothing can drive a wedge as deeply as tattling. Tattling as a means to get the other in trouble is the same as wishing ill will rather than blessing on the brother/sister, causing the bond of trust to be broken. Tattling can be a sign of revenge, or an unfair means of gaining the upper hand in conflict. Whatever the motive, nine times out of ten, it's wrong. Learn to be discerning of what lies beneath the voice of the tattletale.

Taming the Tattletale

"Christopher's not letting me play with the ball!" "Sarah's calling me names!" "Tommy won't let me in the bathroom!" Sound familiar?

Tattling reigns as one of the most common behavior problems among siblings. Parents often simply do not know how to deal with the issue. While some parents are frustrated with their inability to control the problem, others try to rationalize their decision to avoid correction.

"After all," reasons one parent, "if my child is doing something that he ought not do, why does it matter how I find out?"

Another parent says, "If one of my children has been wronged by his sibling, I would rather he come tell me than to fight back."

While these seem like reasonable arguments, they are not biblical. So what's a parent to do? I'm glad you asked. Thankfully, God has given us instructions in his Word, which explain how we are to train our children. Yes, he even talks about tattling! Whew! Isn't it wonderful that we do not have to come up with solutions on our own?

The Scene

David and Brad are playing cars in the family room. While David pushes his red Camaro with t-top on the Hot Wheels track, Brad decides that throwing the cars at a target (i.e. Fluffy, the cat) would be more fun. As Mom washes the dishes, off in the distance, she hears three of the most annoying words a mother can hear, "I'm telling Mom!" followed by, "Tattle-tale, Tattle-tale, I'm not playing with you anymore!"

Charging through the swinging door of the kitchen, the boys come to a screeching halt in front of Mom. David directs a smirk towards his fuming brother, then proceeds to present his case before the maternal judge.

Do you thank David for informing you of his brother's wrongdoing? Do you instruct them both to put away the cars and play with something else? Do you separate them until they forget about the whole issue? Decisions, decisions. A wise mother will base her child-training decisions on God's Word. She will look past the outward behavior of

85

the tattler and concern herself with the issues of the child's heart. She will uproot the weeds of foolishness, plant seeds of righteousness, and teach her child to grow in wisdom.

Step 1

Teach the tattler to evaluate his own heart. It is not the parents' right to judge the thoughts and motives of their children, but they can aid them in evaluating their own hearts. Throughout Scripture, Jesus caused people to evaluate themselves by asking heart-probing questions. Parents can train the tattler by asking thought-provoking questions in the same way Jesus did. By teaching the tattler to determine his own motives, you are teaching him how to "think" like a Christian.

Be sure to ask the questions in such a way that the tattler will take his focus off of the other person and put it onto the sin in his own heart. You might ask, "David, could it be that you are delighting in getting your brother in trouble?" Have David think through the result he is after by "informing" you of his brother's wrongdoing. Require him to verbally express what is in his heart.

Step 2

Teach the tattler to "put off" tale-bearing. Ephesians 4:22 says, "put off your old self, which is being corrupted by its deceitful desires." It is important that you show the tattler precisely what he is doing wrong in accordance with God's Word. You might say, "Honey, did you know that one of the seven things that God hates is one who causes trouble with his brothers?" (Proverbs 6:19).

Remind him of what the Bible says in Proverbs 17:5b, "whoever gloats over disaster will not go unpunished." You might say, "Sweetheart, if you are trying to get your brother in trouble for your own enjoyment then you will get in trouble." In our home, the tattler faces the same consequences as the other child.

Step 3

Teach the tattler to "put on" encouragement. Ephesians 4:24 says, "put on the new self, created to be like God in true righteousness and holiness." It is not enough to rebuke the child for tattling. You must teach him to replace wrong behavior with right behavior. Rebuking the child for tattling without teaching him what he could have done instead would be exasperating for him, and could provoke him to anger.

You might say, "David, Hebrews 10:24 says that we are to 'spur one another on toward love and good deeds.' Rather than tattling, what could you have said to encourage your brother?" If this is a new concept for the child, you may have to offer suggestions like, "Mom says we shouldn't throw things in the house. I don't want you to get in trouble so you better stop." After giving him an example, allow him to think of his own encouraging words.

Step 4

Teach the tattler to practice what he has learned. The training will stick better when the tattler is required to practice the biblical alternative to his sinful behavior. Role-playing is an extremely effective way for the tattler to put his knowledge into practice. Role-playing causes the child to become a "doer" rather than just a "hearer" of the Word of God, equipping him to respond biblically to similar situations in the future.

Lead both children back to the scene of the crime, the family room. Allow Brad to throw (or for the sake of Fluffy, pretend to throw) his car. Tell David to encourage his brother, in a gentle, self-controlled voice, to stop throwing. Require Brad to respond to David's rebuke by refraining from throwing the cars and thanking his brother for his encouragement.

Children learn by repetition. Be willing to work with your children over and over. On those tiresome days when you become weary from taking the time to train them, remember Galatians 6:9, "Let us not become weary in doing good, for at the proper time we will reap a harvest if we do not give up."

There are a few exceptions to the "no tattling" rule. A child should come directly to the parent if another child is not heeding the rebuke/ encouragement, endangering himself, endangering someone else, or destroying property.

PART THREE

Home is Heavenly

When Relationships Are Right

Nine

Living Joyfully
When Your Husband Won't Lead

WHEN I WAS IN THE YOUTH GROUP AT CHURCH, it seemed that all my friends wanted to be a youth director's wife, except for a few more serious girls who wanted to be pastors' wives. Christian girls dream of marrying a Spirit-filled man who will lead daily devotions for their slew of eager-to-learn offspring, consult God through prayer over every decision he makes for his adored family, and be able to quote a Bible verse for every situation. These Christian girls grow to be women who long for a godly husband to love them unconditionally, treat them respectfully, and guide them spiritually. However, when Mr. Spiritual doesn't come riding in on his white horse to carry them away to holy matrimony, many of these women settle for a lukewarm Christian, or worse, a man who doesn't even know Jesus. "After all," they reason, "I can mold him into the spiritual leader."

Then there are women who didn't know Jesus themselves when they married. It wasn't that they were unequally yoked with their man of choice. Spiritual compatibility simply wasn't an issue. Then the wife became a Christian. Suddenly, she is unhappy with her mate, who refuses to join her newly found faith in Jesus and become the spiritual hero of the family. Not only is she unhappy, she's hurt. "Why won't he trust me on this?" "Doesn't he believe me when I tell him what he's missing by rejecting Jesus?"

Thirdly, there are those women who married men who loved Jesus and served him wholeheartedly at one time, but have now become complacent in their faith. The fire burned out. The passion left. He lost his zeal for his first love. Perhaps this is the worst of situations, because the husband who does know Jesus but has turned away from a relationship with him is typically a miserable man. He is a man who swallows conviction and shuns the prompting of the Holy Spirit. His wife feels cheated and deceived by this man who "pretended to be a Christian."

These are common scenarios among Christian wives. One of the saddest parts of the unequally yoked situation is that many women will not allow themselves the joy that is theirs in Jesus without their husband's participation. I do not mean to undermine the wife who desires salvation or a restored faith for her husband. Those are noble desires that should be bathed in prayer. However, I do mean to propose that a wife should base her joy on the hope of Jesus Christ, not on her husband's spiritual condition.

I've witnessed many wives throw away the joy that Jesus offers to pick up anger, depression, and self-pity. They have allowed their expectations of another human to become an idol of the heart. This idol becomes a replacement for the Giver of Joy.

True contentment and joy are found in Jesus alone. Sure, we are to enjoy our marriages. However, if our joy comes from Jesus Christ, we can enjoy marriage whether or not our husbands are the spiritual leaders. Jesus never fails. If our eyes are fixed on Jesus and our joy is rooted in our relationship with him, circumstances are no longer a prerequisite for joy. With Jesus, we can have peace in the midst of turmoil, joy in the midst of trials, and love in the midst of imperfections. How can we do that?

We can be more thankful. Whenever Paul thought about the Philippians, he thanked God. Was he thankful because only good things happened to him when he was in Philippi? Absolutely not. In fact, while preaching the gospel in Philippi, Paul and Silas were dragged away, beaten, bruised, and bound in stocks in the inner cell of the jail (Acts 16). Further, when they finally freed Paul and Silas, the Philippians ordered them to leave. Why was Paul so thankful in the presence of such ill treatment? Was he delirious? Did he forget what had happened? Nope. In 1 Thessalonians 2:2 Paul writes that he suffered and was insulted in Philippi. Bad, painful things happened to Paul in Philippi. Yet, every time he thought about the Philippians, he was thankful.

How was Paul thankful after suffering such depressing circumstances? Simple—he *chose* to be. It wasn't that Paul forgot about all the bad stuff. He followed his own exhortation from Philippians 4:4, "Rejoice in the Lord always. I will say it again: Rejoice." How could he rejoice in the face of hardship? By dwelling on his love for Jesus as well as the love that Jesus had for him. Paul delighted in glorifying Jesus with his life, no matter the circumstances. In light of the joy and hope that were his in Christ, the bad things fell away from his heart and mind. This truth reminds me of the song: "Turn your eyes upon Jesus. Look full in his wonderful face. And the things of earth will grow strangely dim in the light of his glory and grace."[1]

Heaven at home is possible for every wife who has received Jesus as her Lord and Savior. If you are a child of God you have the Holy Spirit living inside you. If you are engaged in a close walk with the Lord, the Holy Spirit will enable you to experience joy in the midst of a not-so-ideal marriage. He will enable you to dwell on things that are true, noble, right, pure, lovely, and admirable, rather than on your unmet desires (Philippians 4:8). Jesus promised, "I have come that they may have life, and have it to the full" (John 10:10b).

If we dwell on memories that cause bitterness, resentment, a critical spirit, and grudges, we are failing to live in the fullness of God. When we submit to his spiritual guidance, and trust his sovereign hands in all the circumstances of our lives, he enables us to be thankful.

There was once a preacher who was known for always opening the worship service with a prayer of thankfulness for the new day that the Lord had given. One Sunday morning the weather was so cold and dreadful that members of the congregation murmured among themselves, wondering how the pastor would express thankfulness for the day itself. The preacher approached the podium grinning from ear to ear and prayed, "Lord, I thank thee that not every day is like this one!"

Being thankful is a command: "Be joyful always; pray continually; giving thanks in all circumstances, for this is God's will for you in Christ Jesus" (1 Thessalonians 5:16–18). Because God is in control, there is always reason to be thankful, no matter how bad the situation. It's all about trusting the sovereignty of God and resting in his truth.

If we are to be thankful, we must look at things from God's perspective. It's easy to praise and worship God when things are going our way, but to give him praise and worship when things are not going our way is to move ourselves aside and exalt him. Funny thing is that when we give up our own wants and focus on glorifying God in our lives, we are filled with joy.

If you are holding on to anger and bitterness because your husband is not the spiritual leader in your home, then you will never be joyful. If you want to increase your joy, regardless of your husband's lack of spiritual leadership, then you must choose, like Paul, to see things from God's perspective. Out of God's love and goodness to you and out of your love and devotion to God, you can choose to glorify Jesus in your response to an unequally yoked marriage.

We can be more confident. If I wanted counsel in how to exercise to be healthier, I would ask my friend Tina, because she is a professional exercise trainer. I would be confident in her counsel because that is what she does. If I wanted to redecorate my home to look as tasteful as homes in *Better Homes and Gardens*, I would consult my friend

Tracy, because she is a professional decorator. I would be confident in her services because that is what she does.

The Bible teaches that God does everything for his own glory. God sent Jesus to earth not just to die for us, but to show us how to live for him and bring him glory. I know that Jesus has begun a good work in me, and I am confident that he will carry it on to completion, because that is what he does. Paul wrote, "being confident of this, that he who began a good work in you will carry it on to completion until the day of Christ Jesus" (Philippians 1:6). I can also be confident that God has always been in control of my life, is in control of my life, and will always be in control of my life: "And we know that in all things God works for the good of those who love him, who have been called according to his purpose" (Romans 8:28).

We must be confident that God is in control of our lives if we want to live at peace and experience joy in the midst of tough circumstances. No matter what we have been through, no matter what mistakes we have made, no matter how badly we have blown it, God is in control of our lives and our circumstances right now. The question you may need to ask yourself is this: "Did God really start something in me in the first place, or was I not serious about my decision to follow Christ?" If, indeed, God did begin a good work in you, he will bring it to completion. What God has started, he will finish. Obedience to God is key. It has been proven true, time and time again, that increased obedience leads to increased confidence that God is at work, which leads to increased joy. One person has written that joy is a by-product of obedience. The longer I walk with Jesus, the more I understand and believe that statement.

True confidence is not found in the sinking sand of a healthy income, well-behaved children, a godly husband, popularity, or our own talents and abilities. It's in the solid foundation of being in Christ. True, unshakable confidence is found in being a child of God.

Confidence is knowing that God is working in our circumstances to accomplish his good and pleasing will.

We can be more loving. Paul experienced joy because he obeyed God and loved the Philippians. You, too, can experience joy in the Lord when you obey God by loving your husband, even when he's not so lovable. You can even experience joy in loving a man who doesn't love you back, simply because genuine joy comes from genuine obedience to God. The more you love your husband to the glory of God, the more your joy will increase. Jesus promised, "If you obey my commands, you will remain in my love, just as I have obeyed my Father's commands and remain in his love. I have told you this so that my joy may be in you and that your joy may be complete. My command is this: Love each other as I have loved you" (John 15:10–12).

Think about the love of Jesus. He demonstrated his love for us by dying on the cross to pay the penalty for our sins. We are told in Hebrews 12:2, "For the joy set before him, he endured the cross." Jesus felt joy in his sacrifice because of his love for us, yet we did not love him. The Bible teaches that while we were his enemies, Christ died for us. Whether your husband loves you or not, whether he is the spiritual leader or not, it doesn't matter. What matters, what brings joy, is if you love him simply because God commands you to love him.

To fail to love your husband because of his lack of leadership, in action or tongue, is to deprive yourself of joy. Amy Carmichael wrote, "Unlove is deadly. It is a cancer. It may kill slowly, but it always kills in the end. Let us fear it; fear to give room to it, as we should fear to nurse a cobra. It is deadlier than a cobra. One drop of the gall of unlove in my heart or yours, however unseen, has a terrible power of spreading all through our family, for we are one body—we are part of another."[2]

C.S. Lewis wrote the following statement about loving our neighbor, which can certainly apply to loving our husbands as well: "Do not waste time bothering whether you 'love' your neighbor; act as if you did. As soon as we do this, we find one of the great secrets. When you are behaving as if you loved someone, you will presently come to love him."[3]

As Paul said in 1 Corinthians 13, the "love" chapter, it doesn't matter what we have or what we do or what we say; if we do not have love it means nothing, and we have nothing. To have joy, we have to be more loving. Paul had great joy when he thought of the Philippians, because he was full of love for them.

One person described joy by saying, "Joy is the enjoyment of God and the good things that come from the hand of God." Too many wives are too bogged down with discontentment to even see the good things God has blessed them with. Too many wives think, "There is no way I can experience joy with my husband's wrong attitude." Remember that Paul wrote to the Philippians while under house arrest in Rome. He actually spent two years chained to a Roman soldier while awaiting trial for his life. Circumstances don't get much worse than that. Yet Paul wrote, "In all my prayers for you I pray with great joy." How was Paul joyful in spite of his circumstances? He kept his eyes on the author and perfecter of his faith. He delighted in believing, trusting, and serving his Lord, and in that, Paul experienced great joy.

Ella Wheeler Wilcox, the author of the following poem, understood that our joy is not dependent on our circumstances.

The Winds of Fate

One ship drives east and another drives west
With the selfsame winds that blow.
'Tis the set of the sails
And not the gales
Which tells us the way to go.
Like the winds of the sea are the ways of fate,
As we voyage along through life:
'Tis the set of a soul
That decides its goal,
And not the calm or the strife.[4]

As believers in the Lord Jesus, we have the Holy Spirit living in us. Therefore, we can be joyful in all situations, even an unequally yoked marriage. But we must choose that joy and pursue it in Jesus. It will become easier to experience joy as we learn to be more thankful, more confident, and more loving—for the sake of our families, for the peacefulness of our homes, and most of all for the glory of God.

Getting Along with Your In-Laws

SAT AT MY DESK FOR OVER AN HOUR staring at my computer screen and thought, *WHY have I committed myself to writing a chapter on in-law relationships?* Feeling incompetent, I could not think of a suitable way to begin. Then it hit me. What better way to start this chapter than with an infamous mother-in-law joke? Smiling at the brilliance of my plan, I did a search on the Internet. This is *not* recommended. It was heart breaking to read the disrespectful, degrading, distasteful, and downright nasty comments written about mothers-in-law. The thousands of off-color jokes and humiliating stories that float around in cyberspace testify to the fact that there is definitely something wrong with the way society views in-laws. I must admit, however, that I did chuckle at this one:

> George went on a vacation to the Middle East with most of his family, including his mother-in-law. During their vacation, and while they were visiting Jerusalem, George's mother-in-law died. With the death certificate in hand, George went to the American Consulate Office to make arrangements to send the body back to the States for proper burial. The Consul, after hearing of the death of the

mother-in-law, told George, "My friend, the sending of a body back to the States for burial is very, very expensive. It could cost as much as $5,000 dollars." The Consul continued, "In most of these cases, the person responsible for the remains normally decides to bury the body here. This would only cost $150 dollars." George thinks for some time, and answers the Consul, "I don't care how much it will cost to send the body back. That's what I want to do." The Consul, after hearing this says, "You must have loved your mother-in-law very much, considering the difference in price between $5,000 and $150 dollars." "No, it's not that," says George, "you see, I know of a case many, many years ago of a person that was buried here in Jerusalem, and on the third day he was resurrected. Consequently, I do not want to take that chance!"[1]

While I giggled as I read this, it is sad that many people would not only giggle, but also relate to George's strong dislike for his mother-in-law. No matter how nasty or nice our in-laws are, it is our responsibility to demonstrate the love of Christ and make every effort to live at peace with them. As we explore what God's Word says, some may be tempted to say, "But you don't know MY in-laws. I've tried everything and there's just no use!" or "That might work for some, but it won't work in my situation." I do not wish to weigh the *shake the dust off your feet* verse against the *make every effort to live at peace* verse on the scale of biblical justice. I do wish to rightly divide the Word of God when it comes to loving others and pursuing peace with everyone.

Certainly, there are many situations in which all attempts to love and honor in-laws will seem to be in vain. However, as hopeless as it may seem, it is always right to demonstrate the love of Christ. Loving the unlovable is one of the most effective ways to show the unconditional love of Christ. It's easy to love people who love us, but to love someone who mistreats us can only be achieved by the supernatural, empowering grace of God. To long for, accept, and live out this grace brings glory to the Father. While glorifying God is reason enough to love your in-laws regardless of their response, there have been many cases where the love of Christ overcame embittered in-laws and resulted in a beautiful relationship.

My dear friend Mary was devastated when her future in-laws kicked up a fuss about her marrying their son. Mary explains:

> Over the years, however, the relationship with my in-laws has grown and changed into a beautiful, precious gift. It has taken time, shared life experiences, a commitment to love and honor each other and refusing to settle for anything less than an authentic and transparent relationship built on mutual honor and respect. To love the parents of your mate is an investment in the health of the family and leaves a valuable legacy for your own children. I will never forget the day Mom came to me with tears in her eyes to say, "We were so wrong. We love you as if you were our own daughter and always will. You are the perfect wife for Dan. Please forgive us." There was nothing to forgive. Somewhere along the way, God changed my heart and theirs.

When it comes to relationships with in-laws, we have a choice. We can choose to wage peace, loving and accepting them just as they are and as God commands, or we can give in to our base human instincts, standing in pride, refusing to forgive or be forgiven. We need to take the higher road of unconditional love. The reward will be a blessed family that honors God.

I asked Mary how she made an effort to love and honor her in-laws when they seemed to not care for her. Mary recalled ten practical ways that she demonstrated her desire to please Jesus in action and attitude toward her disapproving in-laws:

1. Every time they called us I got on the phone and talked with them.
2. I would send cards from time to time—for no particular reason.

3. I listened to my mother-in-law. She and I now joke about it. She says, "Mary and I have a great relationship. She listens to everything I say and then does what she wants."
4. I constantly reminded myself that they are my honey's parents.
5. I chose the attitude of respect and honor and, eventually, the emotions caught up.
6. When they visited, I asked my mother-in-law to help cook meals. She loved it! She loved the fact that I was willing to turn my kitchen over to her, and I loved that fact that she was a great cook.
7. I drew them out by being interested in what they were interested in. I looked at snow skiing pictures, collections of Depression glass, etc. and learned a lot about them and the things they enjoy.
8. I constantly told them how much their son meant to me and thanked them for raising such a great son.
9. I prayed and asked God to change *my* attitude to one of love and acceptance.
10. I vowed to never criticize, even in a joking matter, my in-laws in public. When tempted, I refused to participate in in-law horror stories. Presently, I have none to tell! God's love has covered it all. And now, my in-laws and I not only get along great, we enjoy a special relationship forged through years of chosen obedience.

Your Relationship with Your Husband's Parents

It is important to remember that before he was your husband, he was their baby, toddler, and teenager. A mother, especially, often has a hard time letting go. She was loving and nurturing him way before he grew into the man of your dreams. She hugged him goodbye on his first day of school and wept as she drove away. She cooked his favorite dinner when he had a bad day and let him put the sprinkles on the cookies. She listened to his hopes and dreams even when they were painfully silly, nursed him back to health when he was sick, and tucked him into bed at night. She kissed away his boo-boos and washed away his tears. She cheered at his games, laughed at his jokes, prayed over his struggles, cried over his hurts, and gave much of her life for him. There is nothing like a mother's love for her little boy. Is it any wonder why she gets a little "weird" over another woman taking first place in her son's life?

My mother-in-law is notorious for feeding my husband, Jim, more than he is accustomed to eating when we visit them in "the country." Granted, she blesses us with some down home, country cooking that is simply out of this world. However, she is never satisfied with the amount Jim eats. He should always have more peas or more squash or more corn. Jim could eat ten plates piled two feet high and she would still say, "Let me get you another helpin' of okra, Son."

She doesn't even wait until his plate is empty. She'll take a bite of her own food, glance over at his plate, and ask, "Jim, are you ready for more peas?" She'll take another bite of her food, set her fork down, and while chewing, head for the stove and say, "Let me get you another biscuit, Son." On the way back, noticing that his tea glass is only half full, she'll add, "Oh! you need more tea. You did want tea to drink, didn't you? Because I also made lemonade. Would you like some lemonade?" Everyone at the table acts as though this sort of behavior is completely normal, while I want to stand up in my chair and yell, "Land sakes, woman! Let the man eat in peace!"

It's easy for us wives to get our feathers ruffled. Granted, Jim is a bit on the thin side. He is much thinner than when we married fourteen years ago. It's not the force-feeding that bothers me, as I agree that putting a little meat on his bones is not a bad idea. It's the "Jim, Sweetheart, aren't you eating enough at home?" that gets me. I know she doesn't mean it to be a personal attack on me, but my "territorial" instinct kicks in.

So, what do I do? It's called the defense mechanism, and, I dare say, it's wrong. Human nature, but wrong. I make a special effort to call her on nights when I'm cooking a big dinner. "Hi, Mom, it's me. Whacha doin'? Well, that sounds nice. Me? Oh, nothing. I'm just piddling around in the kitchen. I'm cooking a chicken casserole, broccoli salad, sweet potato soufflé, and homemade yeast rolls for dinner." It's funny the things we'll do to prove ourselves worthy, especially to our husband's mother.

Actually, I tell you this story in fun. If you could witness the wonderful relationship I have with my mother-in-law, you would think I had no business writing this chapter. She is a dynamic lady who loves Jesus wholeheartedly and loves me unconditionally. I am truly a blessed woman to call her my mom, my sister, and my friend. She has always been a trustworthy mentor and faithful confidante. My father-in-law is equal to her in kindness and goodness.

Unfortunately, many are not blessed with in-laws as loving as mine. While this is hard, it is an opportunity to glorify Christ, to give of ourselves for the sake of his righteousness and the benefit of others. As Paul described it, "Though I am free and belong to no man, I make myself a slave to everyone, to win as many as possible" (1 Corinthians 9:19). It is also an opportunity to be joyful. Yes, you read it right. We can be joyful in the midst of hard relationships. It is the trials in our lives that mature our faith in Jesus Christ: "Consider it pure joy, my brothers, whenever you face trials of many kinds, because you know that the testing of your faith develops perseverance. Perseverance must finish its work so that you may be mature and complete, not lacking anything" (James 1:2–4).

We are commanded to love one another. When one of the teachers of the law asked which was the most important commandment, Jesus answered, "Love the Lord your God with all your heart and with all your soul and with all your mind and with all your strength. The second is this: Love your neighbor as yourself. There is no commandment greater than these" (Mark 12:30–31). The translation of the Greek word for neighbor is "close by" or "near to." Another definition is "those closest to us." Who is closer to us than our family? Christ commands us to love our in-laws, with no exceptions.

Perhaps you view your in-laws as the enemy rather than as neighbors. Christ covered this as well in Matthew 5:43–44, "You have heard that it was said, 'Love your neighbor and hate your enemy.' But I tell you: Love your enemies and pray for those who persecute you." One way to show love to them is to do good towards them. "But I tell you who hear me: Love your enemies, do good to those who hate you, bless those who curse you, pray for those who mistreat you" (Luke 6:27–28). Jesus continues in Luke 6:31, "Do to others as you would have them do to you." Notice that he doesn't say treat them as they treat you or as they deserve, but consider how you would like them to treat you and treat them according to that wishful standard. Would you like for your mother-in-law to respect you? Respect her. Would you like for her to compliment and encourage you? Compliment and encourage her. Would you like for her not to criticize you in front of others? Don't criticize her in front of others. To love those who do not love us is to glorify Christ. As we glorify Christ, we will be filled with his comfort and assurance, regardless of the reaction of our in-laws.

We are commanded to live in peace with one another. As Christians we are responsible to "Make every effort to live in peace with all men and to be holy" (Hebrews 12:14a). Living at peace with an in-law might entail abandoning our own rights for the sake of peace. Keeping peace might involve "returning evil with good" by responding in love to harsh comments. For example:

If your mother-in-law asks, "Why do you cook your roast at such a low temperature?"

A strife-provoking response might be, "Because a roast cooked on a low temperature is more tender than a roast cooked at a high temperature" (like her roast).

A peace-promoting response might be, "I would love to have some of your recipes for roasts. I always enjoy your cooking. Perhaps we could cook some of your recipes together."

If your mother-in-law comments, "I don't know why you put that ugly chair in the living room."

A strife-provoking response might be, "Because it's my house and I like it."

A peace-provoking response might be, "I'm sorry you don't like it. I'm really fond of it. Do you have any suggestions as to where it might look better?"

If your mother-in-law says, "You really need to discipline little Tommy better."

A strife-provoking response might be, "That's really not your concern."

A peace-provoking response might be, "I appreciate your encouragement. We are working on some discipline issues."

This isn't to say that you have to do everything your mother-in-law wants you to do. However, respecting her opinions (no matter how different they are from yours) and making every effort to pursue peace at all costs will greatly enhance her respect for you, whether she shows it or not. There is no harm in listening to her opinions and expressing appreciation for her thoughts. Actually, we are commanded to show appreciation; we are commanded to be thankful: "Be joyful always; pray continually; *give thanks in all circumstances*, for this is God's will for you in Christ Jesus" (1 Thessalonians 5:16–18, emphasis mine).

Human weakness is defensive and prideful, but the strength of Christ is shown in humility, submission, and appreciation. When we obey God by promoting peace, one of God's means for working on the heart of another is being put into action. When we are obedient to God by pursuing peace, the righteousness of Christ brings about peace in our own hearts. The Bible promises, "The fruit of righteousness will be peace; the effect of righteousness will be quietness and confidence forever" (Isaiah 32:17).

We are commanded to honor and respect one another. "Honor your father and your mother, as the Lord your God has commanded you" (Deuteronomy 5:16a). This verse goes on to promise that if we honor our fathers and mothers it will go well with us. God always has our best interests at heart. He desires us to be at peace with him by following his commands and honoring him with our lives.

When you married your husband, his parents became your parents, for better or worse. Paul encouraged, "Be kindly affectioned one to another with brotherly love; in honour preferring one another" (Romans 12:10 KJV). The word "affectioned" comes from the Greek word *philostorgos*, which means *tender affection*. [2] To show tender affection to our in-laws honors them and glorifies God. Just as we show tender affection to our children even after they have disobeyed, we are to show tenderness and affection to our in-laws even when we find their actions offensive.

Consider the offensiveness of sin toward the holiness of Christ. I have offended him with my sins in more ways than I care to write about. Yet, in his love, he bore my offensiveness on the cross at Calvary rather than shunning me. The love of Christ never fails. Even if your in-law does not appreciate you, the love of Christ never fails.

One way I show affection to my in-laws is by addressing them with terms of endearment. I call them Mom and Dad. During the first couple of years after Jim and I married, I called them Lee and Thelma. However, I wanted to honor them by accepting them as my parents. It was awkward at first, but looking back now, I see that this simple act of love has drawn us closer together. It identifies who they are to me and acknowledges my loyalty to them as their daughter.

Honoring and respecting our in-laws shows acceptance, which creates trust in the relationship. Trust leads to confidence, communication, and mutual submission. Not honoring and respecting (not accepting) our in-laws tears down trust and leads to defensiveness, insecurity, and suspicion in the relationship.

Ruth, a model daughter-in-law

Ruth was a woman who glorified God by honoring and respecting her mother-in-law. Ruth married one of Naomi's sons, but after a time, he died. Ruth was a free woman. She was still young and could have gone back home and married again, as her mother-in-law pleaded with her to do. However, Ruth's bond with Naomi ran deep. She pledged her love and dedication to her widowed mother-in-law (who had lost her husband as well as both sons) and vowed to never leave her. Even when Naomi urged Ruth to leave, Ruth replied, "Don't urge me to leave you or to turn back from you. Where you go I will go, and where you stay I will stay. Your people will be my people and your God my God. Where you die I will die, and there I will be buried. May the Lord deal with me, ever so severely, if anything but death separates you and me" (Ruth 1:16–17).

Ruth's honor and respect for Naomi were not based on Naomi's actions and attitude. While the name Naomi means "pleasant," Naomi had grown to be a rather unpleasant woman. I imagine it was hard to be around her. She had become a bitter complainer and seemed to have lost her joy in the Lord. "'Don't call me Naomi,' she told them. 'Call me Mara, because the Almighty has made my life very bitter. I went away full, but the Lord has brought me back empty. Why call me Naomi? The Lord has afflicted me; the Almighty has brought misfortune upon me.'" Naomi had become a woe-is-me person. No one enjoys being around a whining complainer and I'm sure Ruth was no exception. Since Ruth's husband had died, she even had a legitimate excuse to abandon her embittered mother-in-law. However,

Ruth was self-sacrificing and others-oriented. She demonstrated her love and commitment to God through her love and commitment to Naomi. As a result, God blessed the sandals off both women. He brought Boaz into their lives. Boaz was a godly, generous, tender man. He was a well-respected, admired, upright (not to mention wealthy) man. In short, Boaz was quite a catch!

Interestingly, the first thing that attracted Boaz to Ruth was the way she honored and respected her mother-in-law. Ruth was a humble woman. She was so shocked that she had attracted his attention that she asked, "Why have I found such favor in your eyes that you notice me—a foreigner?" (Ruth 2:10b). Boaz replied in verses 11–12, "I've been told all about what you have done for your mother-in-law since the death of your husband—how you left your father and mother and your homeland and came to live with a people you did not know before. May the Lord repay you for what you have done. May you be richly rewarded by the Lord, the God of Israel, under whose wings you have come to take refuge." Boaz married Ruth, and their son was the grandfather of David. Ruth's earthly reward was favor in the eyes of the Lord all because she exalted God by honoring and respecting her mother-in-law.

We are commanded to be humble. "For by the grace given me I say to every one of you: Do not think of yourself more highly than you ought, but rather think of yourself with sober judgment, in accordance with the measure of faith God has given you" (Romans 12:3). To presume that we are always right and our in-laws are always wrong is to consider ourselves more highly than we ought. We should always look to honor and prefer others above ourselves. Anything short of this exhibits selfish ambition and conceit, which are displeasing to God (Philippians 2:3–4).

God promises to lift us up when we walk humbly before him: "all of you, clothe yourselves with humility toward one another, because God opposes the proud but gives grace to the humble. Humble yourselves, therefore, under God's mighty hand, that he may lift you up in due time" (1 Peter 5:5–6). God's "due time" is usually not on our timetable, but we can rest assured that his timing is perfect. Walking in obedience to God is exciting, adventurous, and brings about the fulfilling reward of immeasurable peace and joy. Misery is a child of God who is wallowing in pride, unforgiveness, and self-pity. Freedom is found in abiding in him and pleasing him in all that we do.

In order to demonstrate love, peace, honor, respect, and humility, we must recognize our need. Because of our sinfulness, we simply cannot live by these commands apart from Christ. Our need is to acknowledge our ongoing struggle with sin, while taking hold of the holiness of God, which enables us to stand as ones approved. He has freely given us all that we need for life and godliness. What a joy to know that our needs are a pathway to God, not an obstacle that makes him angry or distant. His power is made perfect in our weakness. As we live by the power given to us through Christ, we are transformed into his likeness.

The grace of God breaks through our walls of corrupt and deceitful desires and showers us with love. It's that same grace that enables us to shower others with his love no matter how they act. To love someone who doesn't seem to love us exemplifies the supernatural love of Christ. To give of ourselves without expecting anything back is to love for the sheer glory of God. It is to let his power reign in our lives and transform us into his likeness. Loving in-laws by the grace of God blesses the heart of God. Personally, there is no heart I'd rather bless!

Eleven

Keeping Friendships Christ-Centered

IF I COULD ONLY USE TWO WORDS to define my friend Paula, they would be "southern" and "southern." Paula recently traveled with me to the West Coast, bringing with her the charming lingo that separates Alabama from the rest of our country. Paula doesn't assume, she "reckons." She doesn't laugh, she "gets tickled." She doesn't get angry, she gets "mad as far [fire]." And poverty is defined as "people who don't have a pot to pee in."

Traveling with Paula was an adventure. Being directionally challenged, we spent more time asking for directions than we did enjoying the lovely landscape of southern California. After a mere two-minute conversation with us, the manager of Avis Car Rentals was so concerned about his vehicle that he gave us his home telephone number. As for the Mustang convertible we rented . . . well, let's just say that lowering the top while traveling at sixty-five miles per hour down the San Diego Freeway was not a good idea.

Exhausted from the trip, we sat quietly on the airplane as the flight attendant robotically announced the ABC's of what to do in case of a crash. She had just explained how the seat cushions could be used as flotation devices and how to properly adjust the oxygen masks, when suddenly Paula made up for all of the "ditsy" things we did over the weekend with one profound statement.

"I do believe the flight attendant is misrepresenting the ABC's in this situation," she whispered. "Seat cushions and oxygen masks won't amount to a hill a' beans if this airplane falls 30,000 feet out of the sky. What they ought to be sayin' is A-admit, B-believe, and C-confess, because salvation in Jesus is the only thing that can *really* save these folks if we crash and burn!"

At that moment it struck me how wonderful it is to have friendships where Jesus is Lord. Because Paula and I are sisters in Christ we encourage one another to see Jesus in everyday situations. Something as simple as a flight attendant's ABC safety precautions offers an opportunity for Christian friends to discuss and ponder the goodness of God. And so we did.

We are charged to "spur one another on toward love and good deeds" (Hebrews 10:24), to "encourage one another" (Hebrews 10:25), and to talk about God's commands "when you sit at home and when you walk along the road, when you lie down and when you get up" (Deuteronomy 6:7).

Focusing on Christ in our friendships will bring us closer to one another and closer to him. If we commit ourselves to looking for God in the heartbeat of life, finding him and sharing him with a friend will become as easy as ABC!

Friendships with Believers

The Bible has much to say about the beauty of friendship. Because one of the greatest benefits in friendships is to lift one another up in Christ, our bosom friends should share our love for Jesus. Good advice is, "he who walks with the wise grows wise, but a companion of fools suffers harm" (Proverbs 13:20). We will explore the difference between being a companion of fools and befriending a non-believer for the sake of the gospel (as Jesus did) in the second part of this chapter. For now, let us explore five ways we can exalt Christ in our friendships with believers.

Be encouraging. "Therefore, encourage one another and build each other up" (1 Thessalonians 5:11). An encouraging friend looks out for your best interests by inspiring you with God's Word and pointing you to the hope of the gospel. She will remind you of God's comfort when you are hurting, God's strength when you are weak, God's presence when you are lonely, and God's peace when you are struggling.

When a friend calls and is critical of her husband, do you allow her to slander him (and perhaps join in) or do you offer encouragement in accordance with God's plan for her as a wife? When a friend says, "That Shannon was so rude to me! I don't know who she thinks she is!" do you encourage her to love Shannon anyway and consider that Shannon may be going through a hard time, or do you tell her about the time Shannon was rude to you? The Bible says, "But encourage one another daily, as long as it is called Today, so that none of you may be hardened by sin's deceitfulness" (Hebrews 3:13). Be careful to be in the habit of looking to Jesus when issues like this come up, lest the heart of your friendship be hardened and bound by sin's snare.

Nothing encourages me more than when a friend expresses interest in my interests. When a friend says, "Ginger, how's your book coming along?" I light up like a Christmas tree. Being genuinely interested in the lives of others sends a powerful message of encouragement. My friend Rebecca loves sports. I would rather pull out my toenails than watch a baseball game. However, I try to keep up with who's playing whom and which team she's pulling for. When she calls with the results of the game, I either cheer with her or listen to the details of the devastating mistakes that lost the game. I have to laugh with God. He blessed me with a husband who has as little interest in sports as I do, only to give me a fanatical sports fan for a friend. He's going to stretch me one way or another!

Don't gossip. We are to be "worthy of respect, not malicious talkers but temperate and trustworthy in everything" (1 Timothy 3:11). We are to strive for unity as sisters in Christ. Gossip tears friendships apart: "a gossip separates close friendships" (Proverbs 16:28). I don't know why we are so attracted to gossip. I dare say it is one of the biggest struggles among female friendships. It is also one of the most damaging sins, as it taints the good name of another. Once gossip has been said, it is sure to spread and cannot be taken back.

There was once a young girl who felt terribly convicted for slandering another girl. Trying to ease her guilt, she told her mom what she had done. The wise mom told the girl to gather a bucketful of feathers. The girl was then instructed to walk one mile to the school, dropping the feathers along the way. After the girl had done as she was told, she returned home, not understanding why her mother had asked her to do such a strange chore. Her mother sent her back down the same road with instructions to gather all the feathers and put them back into the bucket. When the girl returned home the second time she replied, "Mom, it was impossible to gather all the feathers. The wind had scattered them all over." The wise mom took the child's face in her hands and gently said, "Just as it is impossible to take back slander before the poison has spread."

When you are tempted to gossip, ask Jesus to show you how to offer encouragement and help to that person. Not only will this put out the smoke before the fire blazes, but it will also turn the temptation into an opportunity to glorify God through helping a sister in need. This is also an effective way to encourage your friends not to gossip. When Suzy starts in with, "Did you hear about why Renee lost her job?" you might reply, "No, but perhaps we should go to Renee and find out what we can do to help. She's probably upset and could use some encouragement and support." By taking the focus off the curiosity of slander and onto the heart of the one being slandered, we honor the will of God.

"Do not let any unwholesome talk come out of your mouths, but only what is helpful for building others up according to their needs, that it may benefit those who listen" (Ephesians 4:29).

Gossiping is a self-righteous way of justifying ourselves. When we criticize others, we feel better about who we are. In doing this, we are justifying ourselves through the comparison of sins rather than the atoning death and resurrection of Christ: "When they measure themselves by themselves and compare themselves with themselves, they are not wise" (2 Corinthians 10:12b).

To say, "Can you believe that Sherry had an affair?" is to say, "I would never stoop so low as to commit adultery, because I am too righteous." Rather than seeking righteousness by analyzing the sins of others, we must humbly admit our own sinful capabilities. Pride says, "I would never do that!" However, given the right set of circumstances, we are all capable of every sinful act. Thankfully, we do not have to justify ourselves before God or anyone else. Christ has atoned for our sins and we stand before him holy and approved. In light of who we were apart from Christ and who we are in Christ, we can build up those who are caught in sin by offering the same grace that has been given to us.

Be helpful. "Suppose a brother or sister is without clothes and daily food. If one of you says to him, 'Go, I wish you well; keep warm and well fed,' but does nothing about his physical needs, what good is it?" (James 4:15–16). The next verses go on to explain that we are to act on our faith. If there is a sister in need, help her. My sister-in-law, Gina is always looking for ways to help a sister in need. Recently, a couple in their church was going through a hard time. The husband had to go away for a couple of months and the wife was left with a two-year-old and her husband's business to run. Gina helped by keeping her two-year-old nearly every day (in addition to her own two babies) for two months. She also took care of their dog and prepared meals for them. Gina is a shining example of faith and love in action.

Helping in little ways can make a huge difference in someone's life. Taking a meal to a new mother, grocery shopping for an elderly friend, or watching a neighbor's children while she and her husband go on a date all show a sense of other-centeredness and please our Father in Heaven. If you don't have much time to offer, be creative. A cancer-stricken friend had to undergo chemotherapy treatments. Several of us took up a collection from all of her acquaintances and paid for weekly maid services for three months. For another friend who needed help, several of us prepared meals and put them in her freezer. Some didn't have time to prepare meals so they gave gift certificates to local restaurants, which was also a tremendous blessing to this family.

Be honest. "Wounds from a friend can be trusted, but an enemy multiplies kisses" (Proverbs 27:6). While a friend's rebuke can hurt, it can protect us, sharpen us, and point us to Christ. Real friends desire what is best for others and will exhibit "tough love" when it comes to putting them back on the right track versus cheering them down a wrong path. It's better to have one friend that will speak truth even when it hurts than a thousand friends who are full of flattery. "Whoever flatters his neighbor is spreading a net for his feet" (Proverbs 29:5). Truth is always good.

There is a difference between being honest and being critical. One is spoken in love, the other in judgment. When we speak the truth in love to a friend (Ephesians 4:15), God uses us to sharpen that person. When we listen to truth that is spoken to us, we position ourselves to be better servants of God. We need to be as willing to accept the truth in love as we are to speak the truth in love. It's not always a pleasant position, but it can result in making us more like Christ, therefore it is most beneficial to listen and accept truth.

Most writers are very sensitive and protective of their work. Most of my female author friends refer to their books as their "babies." In many ways writing a book can be as painful as birthing a baby. Yet the joy of seeing the finished product causes us to forget the painful process. When I reached the halfway point of writing this book, I gave it to my publisher, Tedd Tripp, for review. As we sat down to discuss my work after he had gone over it, I was fully expecting his approval. I had poured my heart into it, and felt confident about the result. Imagine my surprise and disappointment when Tedd began to "speak the truth in love." At that moment, I really didn't want to hear the truth in love; I wanted to hear How Great Thou Art. However, he didn't sing my praises (multiply kisses), he told me how to improve this book and make it more glorifying to Christ. My first thought was *Listen here, Buddy, there are plenty of publishers that would like this book as it is! You can just take your opinion and &%$*@%#!* However, as I began to "take captive every thought," thankfully *before* I verbalized them, I began to accept what Tedd was saying as truth. I silently prayed, *Lord, let me hear you speaking to me through this man. If my re-writing some of this book will bring more glory to you, change my heart.* And so he did. "As iron sharpens iron, so one man sharpens another" (Proverbs 27:17).

In most cases, it's easier to give a rebuke than to receive one. If we think of ourselves more highly than we should, we are more likely to become defensive and/or angry. This sort of reaction is triggered by pride and confidence in oneself. It indicates that we justify ourselves through the acceptance and approval of others. We become defensive out of a refusal to believe that we are anything less than good. With chin up, we shake off the rebuke and decide that the so-called friend is being judgmental.

Then there are those who respond to rebuke with self-pity. They think, "I'll never measure up. I'm always blowing it." This, too, is a response based on self-performance as a means of goodness. It's to believe that righteousness comes from never messing up and from winning the approval of others. This reflects a prideful heart of self-reliance.

The good news of the gospel is that we do not stand condemned in the midst of rebuke. Our approval and righteousness are not measured by our own abilities and performances, but by Christ's. He died so that we would not be condemned. Therefore, we can receive rebuke because we are justified through Christ. We will blow it time and again, but we do not have to defend ourselves or wallow in self-pity. Our hope has nothing to do with whether or not we measure up. Isaiah confirms, "It is the Sovereign Lord who helps me. Who is he that will condemn me?" (Isaiah 50:9a).

Don't judge. "Do not judge, and you will not be judged. Do not condemn, and you will not be condemned. Forgive, and you will be forgiven" (Luke 6:37). I'll be the first to admit that there are times when I am guilty of having a judgmental attitude. I am thankful each and every time God reveals this wickedness in my heart, as I so desire to have a heart like his. I remember one time in particular when God uncovered in my heart the sin of judging others.

As we waited outside the huge mahogany door, nervously wringing our hands, we began to chat. We were both nervous about the same thing, so striking up a conversation was not a problem. In five minutes, I would be meeting with the Senior Director of Acquisitions for Focus on the Family Publishing to pitch my beloved book. When my appointment was over, she would pitch hers.

"So, what's your book about, Lisa?" I probed.

"Well, I haven't exactly written anything yet, but I would like to write a book about my life story," she replied as she glanced down at her hand-written notes on a small piece of paper.

"Next," I heard the appointments director call. I stood and began making my way toward the meeting that I had been dreaming of for as long as I can remember, but not before I smiled sweetly at my new acquaintance, "It was nice meeting you and good luck today."

As I clutched my neatly typed manuscript and well-thought-out proposal, I thought to myself, "That'll never fly, Lady! I've spent eighteen months studying what publishers are looking for and believe me, it's not an unknown woman's life story!"

The next day was Sunday, the last day of the speakers/writers conference. All of the ladies entered the ballroom for a time of praise and worship. Lisa sat behind me. Now, raising your hands or closing your eyes as you worship the Lord is one thing, but hollering out things is another. At least it is in my book. You know, the Ginger Plowman Book of Proper Worship Etiquette.

Lisa was breaking all the rules. Phrases such as, "Praise you, Jesus," "I love you, Jesus," and "Bless you, Jesus" kept springing from her lips and interrupting my own state of worship. I turned around and looked towards the entrance door located in the back of the room and pretended to look for someone (a woman's way of inconspicuously checking someone out). Just as I suspected, Lisa's hands were up as high as they would go, her body swayed, her eyes were closed, and it was obvious that the hollering out wasn't going to stop anytime soon. "Whatever," I thought.

You see, in my sinful, judgmental way of thinking, I always assumed that people who worshiped in this way did it for attention.

After the praise and worship time was over, Lisa was introduced and invited to the stage to share her testimony. My life will never be the same again. I sat in utter amazement as she shared the story of her life. As she testified to the things that Jesus has brought her through, I became aware that she had encountered God in a way that I never have.

"Thirteen years ago I was a homeless drug addict living on the streets of Washington, DC. Today, I am a wife, mother, and anointed woman of God," she said. Although her story involved such things as severe beatings (that she thought she deserved), prostitution, and several other horrible situations, that is not what Lisa focused on.

Her focus was on the forgiveness, the grace, and the awesome power of God.

She described her Heavenly Father as reaching down with his mighty arm and rescuing her from the very depths of hell. She stretched out her arms and her face twisted in a mixture of pain and love as she described her Savior, Jesus Christ, hollering out from a cruel cross with his labored breath, "Lisa, I love you this much." She exalted our Holy God. The Holy Spirit overflowed from her mouth and consumed every lady in that room. Never have I seen his power so evident in a person's life.

Am I saying that Lisa's sins required more forgiveness than my own, making her more thankful? Not at all. Sins do not come in pink, purple, green, or yellow. They are all black in the eyes of God. But the color of gratefulness is expressed in worship. Our songs, our praises, and our prayers paint a glorious picture of worship in which our Lord delights.

As I listened to her praise Jesus for the mighty work he has done in her life, God changed my heart. Shame, shame, shame on me for questioning someone else's love for God and the way they express that love.

If Lisa ever actually writes that book, you can bet your lifesavers I'll be the first one in line to buy it!

Friendships with Non-Believers

I recently heard a young man preach a sermon on the importance of sharing the gospel. His philosophy was that as long as Christians are obeying God by witnessing to the lost, they should not care whether or not the lost accept Christ. He proposed that this attitude takes the pressure off the one sharing the gospel. After all, if we only care about obeying God and not the results of sharing our faith, what do we have to lose? While I agree that the decision of a person to accept or reject the call of Jesus is certainly not the responsibility of the one who shared the gospel, I disagree that the Christian's attitude may be one of not caring. His charge for Christians to not concern themselves with non-Christians who reject Jesus bothered me for two reasons: God commands Christians to care, and God has convicted me many times for *not* caring.

Christians are commanded in Colossians 3:12 to be compassionate. "Therefore, as God's chosen people, holy and dearly loved, clothe yourselves with *compassion*, kindness, humility, gentleness, and patience" *(emphasis mine)*. We are to care, just as Christ cares, for the lost souls of men.

I used to view non-Christians as outsiders. I looked at them as mere projects that I needed to check off my *I shared Christ with them* to-do list. I embraced sharing the gospel of Jesus as my job, and I faithfully did it out of obedience. This "just do it" attitude is definitely in line with my personality. For example, when a turtle makes the dangerous decision to cross a busy road, many people think, "Poor thing." I think, "Stupid turtle." When someone comes to me with a problem, I'm not the huggy, let-me-cry-with-you type. I'm more the factual, "Here's what you need to do so dry your eyes and get on with it" type.

Unfortunately, I must admit, while I had a heart for obeying God in sharing the gospel with the lost, I did not have a heart for the lost. I can recall telling several people about Jesus and not grieving over their negative response to his plan of salvation. God convicted me that I was viewing non-Christians as a type of enemy, an enemy that I needed to conquer in the spiritual war of evangelism. I would faithfully put on my armor, swing the sword of truth at whoever came my way, and walk off the battlefield without giving a second thought to where the wounded fell. I simply counted my efforts as medals toward spiritual heroism.

Jesus doesn't view non-Christians merely as the enemy, but also as victims of the enemy. According to Philippians 2:5, Christians are to have the same attitude as Christ. It took me a while to realize that not having a heart for the lost is just as disobedient as not sharing the gospel. Christ longs to gather his lost sheep. He searches for them and delights in looking after them, "For this is what the Sovereign Lord says: 'I myself will search for my sheep and look after them'" (Ezekiel 34:11). He cares for them (1 Peter 5:7). It is impossible to have the attitude of Christ while not caring for the lost.

In the beginning of this chapter, we saw that a companion of fools suffers harm. Befriending a non-believer for the purpose of sharing the gospel is very different than becoming his companion. Companions are companionable, meaning they are suited for one another socially in their likes and dislikes. Therefore, we are not to be "companions" with non-believers, but we are to befriend them in order to share the good news of Jesus with them.

Jesus befriended non-believers. He befriended and protected a prostitute when no one else would. He went into the house of Matthew, a lying and cheating tax collector, and ate dinner with a gang of sinners in order to subject them to his holiness. "When the Pharisees saw this, they asked his disciples, 'Why does your teacher eat with tax collectors and 'sinners'?' On hearing this, Jesus said, 'It is not the healthy that need a doctor, but the sick'" (Matthew 8:11–12). Jesus came to set sinners free.

As we befriend non-believers for the sake of sharing the love of Christ, it is wise to establish some boundaries. First and foremost, we should never indulge in sinful activities in the name of witnessing. The gospel should be shown with our actions as much as it is spoken with our words. My friend Toma always says, "Your talk talks and your walk talks but your walk talks more than your talk talks." Let the non-believer know up front that you are devoted to Jesus. After all, we are not secret agents, but ambassadors for Christ. "We are therefore Christ's ambassadors, as though God were making his appeal through us" (2 Corinthians 5:20a). Although we should establish who we are in Christ, it is helpful to develop a relationship before bombarding them with Scripture. By showing interest in their lives and getting to know them, we develop trust in the friendship. Keep in mind that a good fisherman hides the hook.

As a fisherman, pray for opportunities to tell others about Jesus. "And pray for us, too, that God may open a door for our message, so that we may proclaim the mystery of Christ, for which I am in chains. Pray that I may proclaim it clearly, as I should" (Colossians 4:2–4). Praying for God to open doors of opportunity to share the gospel has been an exciting adventure for me. I recall one time in particular.

I knew something strange was going on when I couldn't find my seat. After combing the aisles of the Delta airplane two times, seat assignment in hand, I was convinced that I had lost my mind. Was I on the wrong plane? Would I wind up in China, rather than Florida? Would a voice sound over the intercom announcing, "You have now entered the twilight zone"?

Embarrassed that I was not capable of finding my seat, I quietly asked the stewardess for assistance. "No wonder you can't find your seat," she replied after studying my ticket "your seat is in first class, not back here."

She escorted me to the front of the plane, commissioned me to a leather reclining seat, and offered me a Pepsi. Bewildered by my good fortune and intrigued by the many luxurious gadgets in which the first class indulge, I began to investigate my options of play. I resolved to take full advantage of my stroke of luck before the air police realized the mistake and ushered me back to my rightful place.

As I reclined, scanned through the channels on my personal pull-out television, slurped my Pepsi, and started to make a call from my complimentary telephone, the gentleman sitting beside me began to squirm. It was obvious he was sitting next to an amateur first-classer, and an obnoxious one at that.

After answering several of my "What's this thing do?" questions, he glanced back toward the direction from which I had come and stated, "I don't think I've ever seen someone board first class from the back of the plane." I explained that it was some sort of mistake. He didn't seem surprised.

Ten minutes into our conversation, I learned that the man was the vice president of one of the largest Fortune 500 companies in the world, a perfectionist, a philosopher, and a multimillionaire. He was over-confident and extremely intelligent. He knew what he wanted out of life, and he got it—or so it seemed.

I decided that sharing the gospel with this man would be a waste of time. He was simply out of my league intellectually, financially, and socially. I silently vowed to keep the conversation casual. I listened with interest as he told about his line of work. My plan was working.

Then suddenly, the tables turned. He asked me about my occupation.

After telling him about my ministry of writing and speaking on biblical principles, he asked, "So, what brought you to a point of becoming *religious?*" So much for my plan. How could I not witness to this man who viewed my Jesus, the Savior who bled and died for me, as nothing more than a religion? I jumped in with both feet. I shared my testimony of how Jesus rescued a rebellious, promiscuous, alcohol-abusing teenager from the grip of hell and brought her to a place of peace, joy, and contentment.

He listened intently. Then with tears streaming down his face, he asked how to become a Christian. I told him. As the plane landed, my millionaire friend proclaimed through a heavy Latin accent, "You have given me such a gift. I want to do something for you. What is something that you need or want? Whatever you request, I will do it for you."

The temptation was heavy and dark. A new car, a new house, a condo at the beach, and visions of sugarplums danced in my head.

Then another voice interrupted my thoughts. It was a voice from deep within, a voice that I recognized and obeyed. "What would bring me the greatest pleasure is to know that as a result of our meeting, you are seeking the Lord with all your heart. My request is that you read the book of John." With fresh tears and a warm handshake, he gave me his word.

The Lord says, "The harvest is plentiful but the workers are few" (Matthew 9:37). It's a common misconception to think that we must raise support, fly halfway around the world, and sleep in a grass hut on a dirt floor in order to witness to the lost. The harvest is everywhere. It's at the check-out counter in Wal-Mart, standing in line at the grocery or hardware store, in your workplace, on an airplane, and around your kitchen table.

God is able. He will provide the opportunities for those who seek them. Let us be willing to share the gospel of Jesus Christ anytime and anywhere. You might be surprised at where you wind up. I don't know about you, but I could get used to leather recliners and unlimited Pepsi!

Paul tells us in Colossians 4:5–6, "Be wise in the way you act toward outsiders; make the most of every opportunity. Let your conversation be always full of grace, seasoned with salt, so that you may know how to answer everyone." Elizabeth George says, "We have no greater gift to give them than the knowledge of salvation through Jesus Christ."[1]

In realizing these truths, I began to pray for a heart like his. As a result, he enables me to see the lost through his eyes and care for them through his love. I am becoming more and more aware of how precious they are to Jesus. I long to see them embrace their maker, the giver of hope and joy. God is still working on me, but I am thankful that he is making my heart a little more like his each day. Oh, and I simply must tell you . . . I recently pulled my car over to help a turtle cross the road. God is definitely working on me!

Twelve

Encouraging Your Children in Their Relationships with Christ

IN MY BOOK, *Don't Make Me Count to Three*, I instructed parents how to lead their children to Christ and how to encourage them in their relationships with Christ. Here is a short excerpt from what I said:

> All Christian parents long for the day their child receives Jesus Christ as Lord and Savior. "Mommy, I asked Jesus to be my Savior" brings tears to our eyes and joy to our hearts. As parents desiring God's abundant life for our children, we should be overjoyed to hear those words. However, as wise shepherds over the hearts of our children, we should be very cautious.
>
> Leading our children to Christ involves much more than guiding them in a simple prayer. It's living an example before them of what it means to walk with Christ on a daily basis. It's teaching them God's viewpoint in every situation. It's demonstrating forgiveness. It's asking forgiveness. It's living, breathing, and adoring the Word of God in the presence of our children, as well as in their absence . . .

When he sins, encourage him to find refuge in the forgiveness of Jesus. Let him witness you do the same. Teach your sons and daughters the biblical model of admitting sin, being truly sorry for sin, asking forgiveness, and changing sinful behaviors and attitudes.[1]

It is vital that children not view God as "the man upstairs," but as their Father in heaven who desires an intimate relationship with them. "He is a God who is passionate about his relationship with you" (Exodus 34:14 NLT). We must teach them the importance of nurturing their friendship with God.

Encourage them to talk to God. Avoid teaching them to recite cute little rhymes before meals. Rather, have them speak to God from the heart. If you really want to break out of the mold of human tradition, you could inform them that closing their eyes is optional. Teaching children to talk to God with simple everyday words encourages them to be comfortable in their relationship with him. Have them consider the way they talk to their friends about things and assure them that is how God wishes to hear from them. He's not interested in elaborate phrases. He's interested in a sincere heart that desires to know him.

My son, Wesley, came to me one morning and admitted that he had been having a hard time finding the words to pray. I was honest as I admitted that sometimes I do too. I told him that it helps me to pray from the Word of God. Wesley and I took out my Bible, turned to the Psalms and read, "The salvation of the righteous comes from the Lord; he is their stronghold in time of trouble" (Psalm 37:39). I prayed out loud, "Lord, thank you for giving me salvation through your righteousness. You are my stronghold in times of trouble." Then Wesley picked a verse and read, "I will watch my ways and keep my tongue from sin; I will put a muzzle on my mouth as long as the wicked are in my presence" (Psalm 39:1). Then he prayed, "God, help me to not sin when I am talking." We continued with several more verses and Wesley was amazed at how God led him to pray in accordance with his Word.

Another man-made tradition is to pray only at a designated time, a "quiet time." While we certainly have to set aside time to read his Word, praying is something we are commanded to do all the time. Therefore, it is appropriate to pray not just during "quiet time," but also during loud time, sit time, standing time, playing time, and working time.

We can model this for our children by praying out loud throughout the day. Sometimes I pray and they just listen, and sometimes I ask them to offer a short prayer as well. Short prayers throughout the day create more of an awareness of God's presence at all times than long prayers at a designated time.

Encourage them to be honest with God. Wesley went through a spell of confessing every little sin to me. I became concerned, as I did not want to replace Jesus in this area of his life. When I questioned him as to why he felt he had to confess every wrong thought to me, he replied, "I don't like to talk about it with God. I just ask him to forgive me and then I tell you all the details." I had to convince him that it would be better to tell Jesus the details since Jesus is the only one who can clean out his heart. Besides, as a mother, I would RATHER he tell Jesus some of the details instead of me! There are some things that are better left unsaid!

Wesley was afraid to talk to Jesus about the "dirt" because of his reverence for God. He was relieved when I informed him that God *wants* to hear the details because he desires a close friendship with him. Honesty brings about closeness. Was not David referred to as "a man after God's own heart"? I don't think anyone ranted and raved before God with more brutal honesty than King David. God listened and loved David as he accused God of unfairness and betrayal (David was also an excellent repenter!). God didn't strike Jeremiah with lightning when he accused God of tricking him. And Job was called "God's servant" even though he vented his bitterness toward God when his life unraveled. Honesty brings friends closer.

Moses spoke openly, honestly and frankly with God also. In Exodus 33:11, we are told that the Lord spoke with Moses "as a man speaks with his friend." Moses was honest when he protested, "You have been telling me, 'Lead these people,' but you have not let me know whom you will send with me" (Exodus 33:12a). At the end of verse 13, Moses boldly proclaims, "Remember that this nation is *your* people" (emphasis mine). Even after God assured Moses that his Presence would go with him, Moses continued on his rampage as he spoke frankly to the Lord again in verses 15–16, "If your Presence does not go with us, do not send us up from here. How will anyone know that you are pleased with me and with your people unless you go with us? What else will distinguish me and your people from all the other people on the face of the earth?" Rather than getting impatient or angry at the audacity of Moses to question what he just said he would do, the Lord honored the honesty of Moses and said, "I will do the very thing you have asked, because I am pleased with you and I know you by name" (Exodus 33:17).

I am not suggesting that we be irreverent to the Lord, only honest with our feelings. Throughout Scripture, the ones that seemed to be the closest with God are the ones who were honest in their conversations with him. They expressed their fears, disappointments, insecurities, anger, and a slew of other negative feelings and emotions. Likewise, we should also express our thankfulness, joy, pleasure, and all that is good as well.

Personally, the most precious times I've spent with God are the times when I was the most honest. I've cried with him, laughed with him, expressed anger with him, rejoiced with him, worshiped him, questioned him, and left my study desk to fall on my knees before him. He is truly my best friend. What joy there is in knowing our Lord!

Encourage them to read God's Word. Don't assume that your child is too young for the Word of God. God's Word is "living and active" and possesses the power to speak to the heart of any age. When my children couldn't read, I read God's Word to them. Now that they can read, they have a designated time to read their Bibles every morning before we begin school. At the beginning of each school year, we shop together for an age-appropriate devotional book. I let them pick the one they want as long as it has an assigned Bible reading to go along with the devotional.

My daughter, Alex, loves to share what God has taught her through her morning devotional. Simply reading her devotional book and related Scriptures works well for building her relationship with Jesus. Wesley, like me, gets easily distracted when he's reading. Therefore, we have "moved him up" to a Bible study for children where he is required to answer questions in written form to help him comprehend and apply what he has read. This works better for him (and me!). Work with your children by teaching them to read God's Word and apply it to their lives while they are young. Hopefully, it will become a habit as they continue to grow! To know God's Word is to know God.

PART FOUR

Home is Heavenly

When Children Obey

Thirteen

Understanding the Parent's Responsibility

WHEN WE ARE RESPONSIBLE WITH OUR DRIVING, we reap lower insurance premiums. When we are responsible on the job, we benefit with a raise and/or a promotion. When we are responsible in training for a sport, we glean the glory of victory. When we are responsible on our diets, we enjoy a healthier body. While there are many rewards for being responsible, none can compare to raising happy, successful children that love Jesus. I do not believe there is any responsibility as tiring and rewarding as parenting. It's our greatest challenge and our greatest blessing. It can be heart breaking, heart stopping, and heart filling, and will usually jump from one to the other—sometimes in a matter of minutes.

When God entrusts children to our care, he entrusts us with great responsibility. The more responsible we are to train them in the ways of the Lord, the more likely they are to "rise up and call us blessed" (Proverbs 31:28a), which is a grand reward in and of itself. While I can't begin to hash through all the responsibility hats we wear as parents, I would like to highlight a few important ones.

135

We are to point our children to their need for Christ. There is nothing more important than our children accepting Jesus Christ as their Lord and Savior. They are ours for only a time, but we should desire that they be his forever. It's easy to get wrapped up in worldly training and focus solely on their education, socialization skills, and proper etiquette. I do not mean to downplay these things, as they are important to function successfully in the world. However, they pale in comparison to a personal relationship with Jesus and should not take precedence over, or be a substitute for, training in godliness. "For physical training is of some value, but godliness has value for all things, holding promise for both the present life and the life to come" (1 Timothy 4:8). Training them up in the way they should go (Proverbs 22:6) involves teaching them about God's holiness, forgiveness, faithfulness, mercy, grace, and redemption. It's about teaching them the Word of God.

God's Word tells us that we are all sinners in need of God's mercy, grace, and forgiveness: "For all have sinned and fall short of the glory of God" (Romans 3:23).

God's law makes us aware of our need for him. "So the law was put in charge to lead us to Christ that we might be justified by faith" (Galatians 3:24). Since it is God's law that leads sinners to Christ, one of our responsibilities as parents is to make our children aware of God's law through the teaching of his Word.

We are to train them up in the ways of the Lord. No matter what is going on in their lives, God's Word is useful and applicable, for "All Scripture is God-breathed and is useful for teaching, rebuking, correcting, and training in righteousness" (2 Timothy 3:16). Training them up in the ways of the Lord is not about going to Sunday school, church service, and prayer meeting. Those things are good and can add to their spiritual understanding, but living out God's Word in daily life is key for spiritual growth. Attending church while leaving God out of every other aspect of life is nothing more than religion. In speaking against those who practice religion without a personal relationship with him, Jesus said such things as, "Woe to you, teachers of the law and Pharisees, you hypocrites! You give a tenth of your spices—mint, dill and cumin. But you have neglected the more important matters of the law—justice, mercy, and faithfulness. You should have practiced the latter, without neglecting the former" (Matthew 23:23), and "you are like whitewashed tombs, which look beautiful on the outside but on the inside are full of dead men's bones and everything unclean. In the same way, on the outside you appear to people as righteous but on the inside you are full of hypocrisy and wickedness" (Matthew 23:27–28).

Children need to understand that God does not let them into heaven based on their church attendance, but on whether or not they know Jesus Christ in a personal way. We need to be careful that we are not responsible for our children confusing religion with relationship.

We are to train them in righteousness. There is nothing we can do to *make* our children righteous, but we can train them in doing what is right in the eyes of the Lord. We are only *made* righteous through the cleansing power of Christ. However, as we teach our children how to apply God's Word to daily life, we train them to walk in his ways. The psalmist said, "I have hidden your word in my heart that I might not sin against you" (Psalm 119:11).

They must know his ways in order to walk in his ways. One of the best methods of teaching the ways of God is in the context of the moment. Teaching children the Word of God as it applies to their struggles brings them to the awareness that he is living and active in their daily lives. It erases the image of a Santa Claus-like granddad sitting on a faraway throne, and makes them mindful of his presence at all times.

For example, when Michael is scared to go to sleep because of the "sharks swimming around the bed," you might put God's Word in his heart by saying, "Sweetheart, God is always with you. He says, 'Never will I leave you; never will I forsake you' (Hebrews 13:5b). How can we trust God rather than being fearful?" Talking to Jesus together and reading the words of Jesus from the Bible can also reassure your child of his presence.

God's Word is not just to be spoken in church. "These commandments that I give you today are to be upon your hearts. Impress them on your children. Talk about them when you sit at home and when you walk along the road, when you lie down and when you get up" (Deuteronomy 6:6–7). God's Word is to flow freely from our lips and into the hearts of our children. A wise mom "speaks with wisdom, and faithful instruction is on her tongue" (Proverbs 31:26). The more we put God's Word in their hearts in accordance with the happenings of their lives, the more they will see the validity of the Scriptures in a personal way.

We are to teach them the danger of self-righteousness. While it is important to train children in righteousness through the teaching of God's Word, we must also teach them the dangers of self-righteousness. They must understand that their righteousness comes only from what Christ has done for them and continues to do in them. Even when the righteousness of Christ shines through them, it is to his glory and not theirs—because that righteousness is from Christ and not their own deeds. The Bible says, "all our righteous acts are like filthy rags" (Isaiah 64:6a). The purpose of living a godly life is not to become a better, more respected person, but to glorify Christ. Christ is glorified through right living. It's not that he is glorified because we are righteous; he is glorified because our righteousness comes through him. We are righteous through his atoning grace, which covers us. When Christ said, "It is finished," he meant *it is finished.* There is nothing for us or our children to do or not do in order to become righteous; it was all done by the work of Christ at Calvary.

We are to teach them to obey. For children, training in righteousness begins with obedience to parents. "Children, obey your parents in everything, for this pleases the Lord" (Colossians 3:30). Our ultimate goal in teaching our children to honor and obey us is that they might honor and obey Jesus. In a sense, parents are like John the Baptist. John spent his life preparing the way for Jesus. Jesus used John to prepare the hearts of those whom Jesus would later call to himself. In the same way, we are to prepare the hearts of our children for Jesus by calling them to obey us.

A child by nature is foolish: "Folly is bound up in the heart of a child, but the rod of discipline will drive it far from him" (Proverbs 22:15). Discipline is the parent's responsibility. Paul wrote, "Fathers, do not exasperate your children; instead, bring them up in the training and instruction of the Lord" (Ephesians 6:4). Training our children to obey by heeding God's commands demonstrates our own obedience to God.

Our goal in getting our children to obey is not only their outward behavior. While it is a pleasure to be around happy, obedient children, our purpose is to please God, not ourselves. When we focus only on correcting outward behavior while failing to reach the heart, we can cause our children to become like the Pharisees. Jesus said, "These people honor me with their lips, but their hearts are far from me" (Matthew 15:8). Jesus used the analogy of washing the outside of the cup while the inside was still unclean (Matthew 23:25) to describe their hypocrisy.

There are four steps we can take in training our children to obey in accordance with God's Word:

1. Ask them heart-probing questions. In following the example of Christ, we can take the focus off what is going on outwardly and onto the issues of the heart by asking questions such as, "Did you obey or disobey?" Having them verbalize that they disobeyed helps them to take ownership for the sin in their

hearts. "How did you disobey?" helps them to identify exactly what they have done wrong. "How does God want you to obey?" We taught our children to answer this question with "All the way, right away, and with a joyful heart," which covers complete obedience.

2. Teach them what to "put off." In Ephesians 4:22, we are told, "You were taught, with regard to your former way of life, to *put off your old self*, which is being corrupted by its deceitful desires" (emphasis mine). The outward behavior is driven by what is in the heart. Therefore, we must reach past the outward behavior and pull out the issue of the heart that the outward behavior is drawing from.

For example, blame shifting or making excuses for wrong behavior draws from pride, which is a heart issue. Not sharing draws from selfishness. Whining draws from a lack of self-control. No matter what the behavior is, God has provided us with the information we need. "His divine power has given us everything we need for life and godliness through our knowledge of him who called us by his own glory and goodness. Through these he has given us his very great and precious promises, so that through them you may participate in the divine nature and escape the corruption in the world caused by evil desires" (2 Peter 1:3–4).

3. Teach them what to "put on." Paul goes on to say in Ephesians 4:23–24, "to be made new in the attitude of your minds; and to *put on the new self*, created to be like God in true righteousness and holiness" (emphasis mine). It is never enough to train our children in what not to do. We must train them in what to do. Biblically, we must always follow through with training them in the biblical alternative to their sinful behavior. It is most beneficial not just to tell the child what to put on, but to have him actually do it.

For example, if a child is whining, ask a question such as, "Honey, are you asking for your baby doll with self-control?" and perhaps inform her, "God wants you to have self-control, even with your voice. I'm going to have you wait five minutes, then you may come back and ask for your baby doll the right way." The most important part of this training is having the child come back and practice the biblical alternative to the wrong behavior by asking for the baby doll with self-control. That is teaching her to "put on" the righteousness of Christ.

4. Follow through with consequences for direct disobedience. This is the hard part. It is never fun to spank our children. I never believed my dad when he said, "This is going to hurt me more than it hurts you" until I began spanking my own children with a heavy heart. However, spanking is part of God's ordained method for teaching children to obey: "Do not withhold discipline from a child; if you punish him with the rod, he will not die. Punish him with the rod and save his soul from death" (Proverbs 23:13–14).

We are to spank our children in love. It would be better to refrain from spanking altogether than to administer a spanking in unholy anger, which is to sin against God and your child. Take a few minutes to pray through your anger while your child waits in his/her room if you feel your motives are in question. Before I administer spankings, I like to say, "I love you too much to allow you to disobey and live foolishly."

We are to pray for our children. Since I have written at much more length on this in *"Don't Make Me Count to Three!"* I will quote a few brief excerpts:

> No matter what stage of life our children are in, the most important thing we can do is to pray for them. Whether they're in diapers, danger, love, rebellion, or a sports car, our most powerful and effective tool in parenting is fervent prayer over every aspect of their lives.

Study your children and know what is going on in their lives so you will know how to pray specifically for each one of them. Find verses from God's Word relating to the issues they are facing. Ask your children how you can pray for them. Pray the Word of God for your children (Hebrews 4:12).

Pray out loud with them. Pray often. Pray conversationally as though you are talking to someone in the room with you (without a lot of "thees" and "thous" or churchy-sounding phrases that are hard for children to understand). Pray everywhere—indoors, outdoors, driving in the car, feeding the cat—so your child realizes his Heavenly Father is always available.[1]

Encourage prayers that seek to glorify God, rather than ones that merely state a list of requests. Children as well as adults often pray, "Thank you, Jesus, for dying for my sins." That's fine, but shouldn't we acknowledge why he died for our sins? He died on the cross so that we might honor him, glorify him, and point others to him. Paul said that Christ endured the cross "so that the Gentiles may glorify God for his mercy" (Romans 15:9). Yes, Christ died for us, but first and foremost, he died to bring glory to the Father. It's not about us; it's about him.

Every November our church has a "Thanksgiving service" where volunteers stand and thank God for something he has done in their lives. Most of the thanksgivings revolve around answered prayers for health, finances, and blessing after blessing that God has graciously bestowed. It's not that these thanksgivings are bad. It's that they assume that Christianity is all about *us* and what God has done and is doing for *us*. I think it would be neat one year to express our thanksgivings as we answered such questions as, "How was God glorified this year? How was God exalted this year?" What a different perspective we would have if we focused on blessing God as well as God blessing us. We mustn't long for God's blessings more than we long for his glory.

Talking So Your Children Will Listen

O YOU EVER GET THE FEELING that your children aren't listening to your instructions? You have just offered an ocean of wise counsel but your little sailor seems to be floating in an entirely different sea. You recognize the warning signs: glazed over eyes, a robotic nod of the head during inappropriate segments of the conversation, an occasional "uh, huh," and that irritating sigh of impatience that says, "How much longer is this woman going to talk?"

Teaching children to listen to advice and accept instruction is of vital importance for their character development. Solomon reiterates the wisdom of heeding instruction in Proverbs 19:20, "Listen to advice and accept instruction, and in the end you will be wise." The connection between wisdom and listening to counsel saturates the pages of the Bible, reminding parents of the responsibility to diligently train their children.

God has placed parents as the authority over their children in order to instruct them in wisdom. The child who is not submitting to the counsel of his parents is acting foolishly. He is rejecting the jurisdiction of God. A child who never learns to listen and heed the counsel of his parents can grow into an adult who has trouble listening to and obeying his Heavenly Father.

All parents desire their children to listen and follow their instructions. Yet many parents are frustrated by their children's lack of attentiveness. The problem often lies in the parent's inability to communicate effectively. Consider the following guidelines:

Understand the art of communicating. As parents, we may believe that we are good communicators if we are able to verbalize our thoughts and feelings to our children in a way they can comprehend. As Christian parents, we may think that if we administer verbal instruction based on God's Word, we are training them appropriately.

However, effective communication involves listening as much as talking. It entails drawing out the thoughts and feelings of our children. In Proverbs 20:5, Solomon says, "The purposes of a man's heart are deep waters, but a man of understanding draws them out." Rather than talking "to" our children, we must learn to talk "with" our children. True communication is not a monologue; it's a dialogue.

Some children are quick to share their hearts while others need prompting to open up. Asking good questions can help get the lines of communication going and identify the issues of the heart. "What were you feeling when you hit your sister?" or "In what ways is hanging out with this friend a wise decision?" or "How is your attitude showing thankfulness and contentment?" or "How can you please Jesus in this situation?"

When we always talk and never listen, we can miss opportunities to look into the hearts of our children. Also, by always telling them right from wrong rather than discussing it, we can cause them to become handicapped in discerning issues of the heart. By training them to evaluate their own hearts, we teach them to grow in wisdom and govern their own behavior in accordance with God's Word. By asking questions rather than pointing everything out, we exercise their ability to "think" as a Christian.

Decide what and how much to communicate. Avoid discussing more than one issue at a time. For effective instruction, focus your correction on the most important aspect that needs immediate attention. Resist the temptation to use one teachable occasion to unload both barrels. Look for other occasions to address unrelated concerns.

Be sensitive as to when enough said is enough said. Once you have conveyed the necessary instruction, correction, or advice, shut off your fountain of wise words. Do not become a leaky faucet that drips frustration into the heart of your child. Put the issue to rest and allow the Holy Spirit to work.

Beware of the dangers of scolding. To scold is to demonstrate a lack of self-control by verbally lashing out with an aggressive, boisterous tone of voice. We should make every effort to avoid scolding our children. Scolding is an angry response and always represents an unrighteous attitude, a loss of temper, and a lack of self-control. Biblical communication reflects control of temper and carefully measured words spoken in a normal tone of voice. Speaking harshly can provoke your child to anger and cause him to resent rather than repent. We are warned in James 1:19, "For man's anger will not bring about the righteous life that God desires."

Scolding says, "I told you to stand right beside me in the grocery store! Why can't you just do what I say? You never listen to me and I am really getting tired of it!" Careful instruction says, "Sweetheart, I told you to stand beside me in the store. Have you obeyed or disobeyed? God says that children are to obey their parents. Honey, I love you too much to allow you to disobey."

If you are angry, take time to pray. Have your child wait in his room for a few minutes while you ask God to make your heart right. "The heart of the righteous weighs its answers, but the mouth of the wicked gushes evil" (Proverbs 15:28). Your child will be more receptive to your instruction if you communicate with a gentle, loving, and self-controlled voice.

Make eye-to-eye contact. With young children this is extremely important. Bending down to their level and making eye-to-eye contact insures that you have their undivided attention. Small children can become so engrossed in the activity at hand that they tune out the world around them. Parents need to re-direct their child's attention to the voice of authority before giving instructions. Eye-to-eye contact eliminates any confusion as to whether or not the child heard your instructions.

Making eye-to-eye contact benefits older children as well. Taking time to stop what you are doing speaks volumes to his heart. Refrain from what you are doing when an opportunity for instruction presents itself and look into the sweet eyes of your child. Offering him your full attention communicates that he is important to you.

Choose the right time and place. It is unnecessary and inappropriate to rebuke children in front of others. Jesus taught, "If your brother sins, go and show him his fault in private; if he listens to you, you have won your brother" (Matthew 18:15 NAS). Children are more attentive to our instructions when they are not suffering from the embarrassment of being reproved in front of other people, especially their friends.

A child who has been reproved in front of others will focus on the embarrassment rather than the sin in his heart. Your goal is not to embarrass or humiliate him, but to encourage a right relationship with God through repentance. If other people are near by, respect your child's feelings by escorting him away from others before giving the reproof. If this is not possible, quietly instruct him in his ear.

Choose the right words. When children succumb to temptation, we must not cushion their fall by trying to soften the reality of their sin. Understanding that it is God's wisdom from God's Word that will bring about a change of heart will motivate us to use the Scriptures for teaching, rebuking, correcting, and training our children in righteousness. If we want to truly penetrate the hearts of our children, we must speak the truth of God's Word: "For the word of God is living

146

and active. Sharper than any double-edged sword, it penetrates even to dividing soul and spirit, joints and marrow; it judges the thoughts and attitudes of the heart" (Hebrews 4:12).

When Danny speaks disrespectfully, avoid saying, "You're acting *ugly.*" Use God's words in order that he might be convicted: "Danny, you are being *disrespectful* and *dishonoring* me. It will not go well with you if you dishonor me like that. Now, try that again and this time, speak in a way that shows respect." It's not necessary to preach a sermon. The wording you just read is based on God's Word (Deuteronomy 5:16), but spoken in a way that comes naturally to me. God's Word can be communicated effectively by simply addressing the issue biblically, yet paraphrasing in your own unique way of talking.

When Angela says "no" after you tell her to put the remote control back on the table, avoid saying, "You are being *stubborn,*" or excusing her behavior with, "I wish you weren't so *strong-willed.*" Use God's words in order that she might be convicted: "Angela, you are being *disobedient.* When you disobey me, you are disobeying God and living foolishly. God says that children are to obey their parents (Colossians 3:20). It's my responsibility to train you to live wisely."

When Zachary says he didn't cut hair off the cat while he is sitting next to the scissors, clutching Garfield's detached whiskers in his fist, don't wimp out by saying, "It's not nice to tell a *fib.*" Use God's words in order that he might be convicted: "Zachary, you are telling a *lie.* The Lord hates a lying tongue (Proverbs 6:16–17), but delights in those who are truthful" (Proverbs 12:22).

Avoid the temptation to sugarcoat sin. Call it what God calls it and allow the Holy Spirit to work through biblical terminology (God's words) rather than worldly terminology (man's words). As you read earlier, God uses the law of his word to bring about conviction and to lead sinners to Christ. Paul wrote, "So the law was put in charge to lead us to Christ that we might be justified by faith" (Galatians 3:24). Let the light of God's Word shine into the hearts of your children in order that they might come to Christ.

Fifteen

Demonstrating Grace in Parenting

HE IDEA FOR THIS CHAPTER was sparked by my sweet friend Valerie Shepard. Valerie and I spoke together at a conference, and I was so intrigued by her testimony on grace in parenting that I asked her to share it in this book. Like many of us, Valerie wove her personal ideas for parenting around her own agenda rather than depending on the grace of God. Because of Valerie's transparency in sharing her misconceptions of "godly parenting" as well as the lessons God taught her about his grace, perhaps we can glean from her wisdom and avoid some of the unnecessary heartache she endured. Here's her story:

> My greatest desire was to be a perfect mother, and have a home that exemplified order and peace, along with love and laughter. My struggles at keeping a routine, making sure Walt led daily family devotions, as well as keeping up my own personal devotions, became more and more just that—STRUGGLES! I wanted to make my children happy, and I found myself giving in to the children's whines or whimpers, without realizing how that would become more and more of a problem.
>
> Having a harmonious mealtime was one of my goals, but the reality of my sin, as well as that of my family's, was a complete shock to me.

149

Growing up in a home as an only child with a godly mother, I had not experienced sibling rivalry, or interruptions, or irritations of any sort. My mother and father [Jim and Elisabeth Elliot] had exemplified serious commitment to Christ, putting obedience to him above all feelings, and viewing suffering for him as a privilege. I had no siblings to be jealous of, or to follow in competition, so when my own children began to show those traits, I was unprepared.

Confidence in my heritage led me to trust in myself . . . surely I could do this because of who I was. Surely my sincere desire to be a perfect mother would make me one! So I wrote out complicated charts and schedules of meals, chores, school times, meal times, family devotions, etc. At one time, I even tried to have a "ticket system" with rewards and punishments given through tickets for every good behavior as well as tickets taken away for every infraction. I thought my high expectations would win out, and the ideal of the harmonious loving family would follow my hopes through my charts.

Well, it didn't work as I had earnestly hoped. I loved my ideals more than I loved God. I thought if I just had enough discipline and routine, the children would all want to be sweet, loving, and obedient. But I couldn't follow my own rules! I berated myself regularly because I couldn't, and I began to feel like such a failure. One day I would work really hard to follow my rules, give consequences, and punish properly. The next day I would either have completely forgotten what I said would be a consequence, or I would make excuses for why I shouldn't give the proper punishment. My children's whines would win, and I became more miserable. I began to be more frustrated, more discouraged with my own lack of discipline, and more fearful that my children would not grow up to be godly adults, though I couldn't articulate my fear. Now let me make one thing very clear: Rules are good to follow, and they help to train up children in righteousness, but they are not the ultimate cause of godliness.

My dear husband began to tell me that we must raise our children in *faith* in a covenant-keeping God, rather than in fear. I didn't understand him. Walt would also say that I needed to be more thankful for them, but I didn't listen. I kept thinking that if we could both be more disciplined, things would be easier, and our children would be "sweeter." I lectured Walt on how he needed to get up earlier, pray more, read the Bible more regularly to them. Of course, the lectures didn't help things at all, and only brought tension and "furrowed brows." I didn't realize how much I was trying to control him as well as the children, for my own sense of accomplishment.

When I began to listen to my husband, to pray more for him with thankfulness, to be more thankful for our children, and to beg God to help me say no to my own selfishness (which is what caused my inconsistencies in punishments), a new understanding began to dawn on me. I started to see his grace as more important than my trust in my good charts and rules. I realized that raising the children with his grace meant a humble, continual dependence on God's strength and energy to flow through me. It meant humbling myself under God's mighty hand and trusting his Holy Spirit to love through me even when the children were hard to love because of their recalcitrance.

I found the most wonderful verses that completely revolutionized my thinking on parenting. First, I found Isaiah 30:15–18, which exhorts us to return to him, to repent of our own ways of doing things, and to look to the God who longs to have compassion on us. His promise is that we will find rest and salvation when we humble ourselves in returning to him, and that he will lead us with careful guidance, as we call to him and trust in him. My own ways had not been working, because I had been too dependent on my own strength and my own ideas. I had to repent of focusing on my ideals, which had really become idols.

I also found in 2 Corinthians 9:8–11, marvelous promises that he would give me the grace to do every good thing that needed to be done in our home. I was amazed that for so many years I had been struggling to "do it right," forgetting to call upon God, or to depend on him for the grace needed when I failed, or when any of my family failed.

The main principle of grace is that it's not about how well we do in our Christian lives, but how marvelous are his forgiveness and mercy for our failures. I had thought that because of my heritage, surely I should be able to do the work of parenting with success . . . in other words, it would be a marvel to many that Walt and Val Shepard had raised such godly children. Look at us!! No, God's grace and his glory are what we should be focused on, not ourselves or our own accomplishments.

The gospel has to make a daily difference in our walk through whatever circumstances or weaknesses or personalities we have. I saw how I needed to walk in repentance throughout the day. Some people are more disciplined than others, they seem to have the will to persevere and discipline consistently, without the struggle that I had of forgetfulness or giving in to the children's desires. I couldn't compare myself to those people, but rather, I had to accept who I was in the Beloved (Ephesians 1:6), because he accepted me! I found that God's grace was sufficient for all my failures, my inconsistent training, and that it was his grace that would draw my children to himself. I could not make my children godly simply by loving them or training them perfectly, but it was God's ultimate responsibility to change their hearts into desiring his righteousness. Hallelujah! I was NOT their owner or controller! God was to be trusted absolutely for their growth in character, and for their salvation.

We can all learn from Valerie's honesty. It's easy to become caught up in our own agenda rather than the goodness and grace of God. While consequences should not be disregarded when rules are broken, grace presides in God's command for us to be humble, patient, loving, forgiving, accepting, and merciful at all times (Galatians 5:22–23).

There are some practical ways we can saturate our parenting with God's grace, but first and foremost, we must realize that we cannot adhere to these practical applications of Scripture in our own strength. God's commands are broken because we are sinful. We simply cannot keep them. The good news of the gospel is that we do not have to deem ourselves failures when we blow it. Christ has redeemed us. Therefore, we do not despair in our failures, but rejoice that we are blameless in Jesus. When we fall, we get up and push forward because Christ has already won the battle of sin for us. When we fall again, we get up and push forward because Christ has redeemed us and made us clean. When we fall again, we get up and push forward because we have inherited the righteousness of Christ.

Nothing can separate us from the love and grace of God. Realizing that Christ alone enables us to keep his commands, and covers us when we don't, we can consider the following practical suggestions for applying God's commands in our parenting:

Acknowledge that we aren't perfect. There is no such thing as a perfect parent. Our attempts at good parenting are only made successful by God's grace.

I've known many people who grew up with alcoholic, abusive parents, who by God's grace alone became faithful men and women of God. I've also known quite a few people who grew up under the love and training of godly parents, but became estranged from the Lord. Certainly, God uses us as tools for reaching the hearts of our children, but who they become is based solely on their personal response to God's calling and his transforming power in their lives, not on our performance as parents. Understanding that our children's outcome is a result of God's grace protects us from glorifying ourselves when they turn out well and releases us from the guilt of imperfect parenting when they turn out badly. Whether or not we enforced the right rules or administered the right consequences dims in comparison with the working of God's grace in the lives of our children. Paul said it best: "I do not set aside the grace of God, for if righteousness could be gained through the law, Christ died for nothing" (Galatians 2:21). Christ has already justified us. We cannot add to or take away from that justification by succeeding or failing. We mustn't carry the burden of self-reliance as if our salvation, or the salvation of our children, depended on it. We are freed from the burden of perfect parenting through Christ who is all that we need for life and godliness.

On the flip side, our children aren't perfect either. In Romans we are told, "For all have sinned and fall short of the glory of God" (Romans 3:23). Therefore, while we shouldn't excuse sinful behavior, we also shouldn't be surprised when our children sin. Rather than being shocked or angry, we can see them as being molded into the image of Christ. We can acknowledge them as being perfected in Jesus. After all, if that's how God views them, should we view them as anything less?

Exemplify humility. Where there is humility there is grace. In the book of James we are told, "God opposes the proud but gives grace to the humble" (James 4:6b). When we are willing to humble ourselves as parents, God's grace is unleashed in our parenting.

One powerful way to express humility is by seeking forgiveness from our children when we have sinned against them. I have failed many times at faithfully training them in the ways of the Lord. When my children have been obedient for long periods of time, I tend to get slack in my parenting. I begin to let random acts of disobedience slide rather than faithfully training them in accordance with God's Word. Before I know it, my disobedience has allowed little weeds to grow strong and overtake the harmony in our family. At these times I have to ask my children to forgive me. I will say something like, "Kids, I have not been faithfully training you to obey in a way that pleases God. I've been allowing you to disobey in these areas (I list the issues of disobedience). Please forgive me for not training you in the wisdom of God." Then we go over the standard and start fresh. Thankfully, God is a God of second chances . . . and third chances . . . and fourth chances . . . and so on!

God honors humility by pouring out his grace. When we model humility before our children, we offer them a front row seat at God's grace in action. It is also a good idea to let them see humility demonstrated in relationships outside our families. The times I have allowed them to witness my failure and repentance in situations that do not directly involve them are the times my children seem most receptive to listening and seeking to understand God's ways—more so than when I have brought their own downfalls to their attention!

Another way God uses humility in my own life to draw the hearts of my children is by giving them the freedom to rebuke me for sin. One of my biggest struggles is my attitude during school. When God called me to home school, I prayed, "Lord, you must have mistaken me for one of your other children. You know I hate school. You know I barely made it through high school, and was thrilled when matrimony rescued me from the depths of . . . college. You know I struggle with patience, and would rather undergo the worst torture treatments than twelve more years of school! Pah-leeeeaaase don't do this to me!" Well, he did.

I can honestly say that I am thankful for being called to home school. He has used home schooling to make me more like him. Striving to walk in humility and desiring to not sin against God and my children, I have given my children the freedom to ask, "Mom, is your attitude pleasing to God right now?" Yikes! It's humbling, but it keeps me accountable. Demonstrating humility in this way provides occasions for the grace of God to overcome my sins in the presence of my children.

Demonstrate unlimited patience. Demonstrating patience when our children sin must not be confused with neglecting the administration of consequences. While God's patience with his children is seen over and over throughout Scripture, it is not to the detriment of consequences. God evinces patience as he teaches, waits for, and admonishes his children.

When Adam and Eve rebelled against God, who spared no expense in giving them every good thing, lightning didn't strike them dead. They deserved to be swallowed up by the earth, but in his great mercy and patience, God administered consequences while extending their lives for hundreds of years. In his sovereignty, God knew that Adam and Eve would continue to sin and produce little baby sinners, yet in his patience he endured their sins and did not wipe them from the earth right then and there.

Although he was angry, he put up with the sinful behavior of the stiff-necked Israelites, who had sinned against God in every way imaginable. Luke said, "he endured their conduct for about forty years in the desert" (Acts 13:18). Out of his great love, he was patient with the rebellious Israelites, delivering them over and over. The psalmist stated, "Many times he delivered them, but they were bent on rebellion and they wasted away in their sin. But he took note of their distress when he heard their cry; for their sake he remembered his covenant and out of his great love he relented" (Psalm 106:43–45). God was patient with them, but still allowed them to suffer the consequences of their sins. We can extend patience to our children only by the grace of God. The Scriptures tell us that it is by his righteousness that his character is manifested through us: "This righteousness from God comes through faith in Jesus Christ to all who believe" (Romans 3:22a). We can be patient while training our children over and over again (often in the same lessons) and still be faithful to administer consequences.

Patience is to be manifested at all times, not just when our children disobey. It's shown in allowing them to do things on their own rather than doing things ourselves to save time. I have found myself cleaning Alex's room for two reasons: I can clean it better; I can clean it faster. However, when I let impatience control my actions, I miss opportunities to teach her responsibility and let her develop skills. If we complain because the bed still has wrinkles after they have made it (or in Alex's case, still has stuffed animals under the sheets), we risk exasperating them. To show patience might be to endure the not-so-perfect bed for the day and say, "You sure are being responsible making your own bed!" The next morning you might consider offering tips as you assist her in making the bed.

Personally, my level of patience varies in accordance with whether or not I spend time with Jesus before my day begins. On the days that I fail to spend time with him, I am not so slow to anger and my patience runs thin. However, when I ask him to fill me and manifest himself through me, I am much more patient and loving to my family. In my own strength I am a grouchy sinner, but through his strength I am a not-so-grouchy sinner who reflects his patience and love. Paul reminds, "I can do everything through him who gives me strength" (Philippians 4:13).

While showing patience certainly benefits those around us, allows God's love to radiate through us, and makes for a more peaceful home, the main reason we exhibit patience is that it pleases God. When

Paul earnestly prayed for the Colossian Christians to please God, he included patience:

> For this reason, since the day we heard about you, we have not stopped praying for you and asking God to fill you with the knowledge of his will through all spiritual wisdom and understanding. And we pray this in order that you may live a life worthy of the Lord and may please him in every way: bearing fruit in every good work, growing in the knowledge of God, being strengthened with all power according to his glorious might so that you may have great endurance and patience, and joyfully giving thanks to the Father, who has qualified you to share in the inheritance of the saints in the kingdom of light.
>
> (Colossians 1:9–12)

Will we always be patient no matter what? Certainly not. However, when we blow it in our own strength, we go right back to clinging to Christ. We move forward in hope. God will convict us when we sin, but he sees us clothed in the perfection of Christ, therefore, we are not condemned. "We are hard pressed on every side, but not crushed; perplexed, but not in despair; persecuted, but not abandoned; struck down, but not destroyed. We always carry around in our body the death of Jesus, so that the life of Jesus may also be revealed in our body" (2 Corinthians 4:9–10). Everything that we are not, he is, on our behalf.

Offer unconditional love and forgiveness. Just as the Father's love for us is not based on our behavior, neither should our love for our children be based on their behavior. It makes me shudder to think of God's love and forgiveness for me being measured in accordance with my actions. I am encouraged by Paul's words: "But where sin increased, grace increased all the more, so that, just as sin reigned in death, so also grace might reign through righteousness to bring eternal life through Jesus Christ our Lord" (Romans 5:20b–21). It is through the sacrificial death of Christ that we are forgiven, not our attempts at better behavior: "But God demonstrates his own love for us in this: While we were still sinners, Christ died for us" (Romans 5:8). Christ loved us so much that he sacrificed himself in order to remove the one obstacle that could keep his love from us—sin. By his grace, he lets nothing stand in the way of his love for us.

Because of Jesus' great love, and the price he paid for that love, we can love and forgive one another. To consider what he suffered in order that we might be forgiven, sheds light on why it is extremely self-righteous to withhold forgiveness from one another. It's to say that we are righteous but Jesus is not. We are commanded to forgive: "Forgive as the Lord forgave you" (Colossians 3:13b).

When we repent, he forgives us completely. The Scriptures assure, "As far as the east is from the west, so far has he removed our transgressions from us" (Psalm 103:12). We mustn't pull out a list of past sins when we are upset with our children. We are told in Corinthians that love keeps no record of wrongs: "Love is patient, love is kind. It does not envy, it does not boast, it is not proud. It is not rude, it is not self-seeking, it is not easily angered, it keeps no record of wrongs" (1 Corinthians 13:4–5). Therefore, we are to forgive and forget, offering a clean slate after each sin, just as the Lord offers us.

When we repent, he forgives us instantly. We mustn't fall into the temptation of harboring unforgiveness by giving our children the silent treatment or the cold shoulder. To withhold forgiveness for any length of time is to sin against God and our children. Obviously, sin is disappointing, but we must let the grace of God be demonstrated in our forgiveness. To not forgive because of feeling wounded or betrayed or embarrassed is selfish. It's to consider ourselves more important than others. Jesus modeled instant forgiveness under the hardest circumstances imaginable. Even as he was being nailed to the cross, he cried out on behalf of the ones crucifying him, "Father, forgive them, for they do not know what they are doing" (Luke 23:34). Is there any forgiveness more instant than that? When the thief on the cross next to Jesus sought mercy, Jesus immediately said, "I tell you the truth, today you will be with me in paradise" (Luke 23:43). What an example of love and forgiveness

Jesus set for us that day at Calvary! In following the example of Christ, we need to forgive when our children repent, being careful not to keep a record of wrongs, withhold affection, or "stew" over their sins. Our tendency is to hold grudges or feel sorry for ourselves when we have been wronged, but we have been given the nature of Christ, who loves and forgives completely. Because he lives in us, we can forgive.

Accept the uniqueness of each child. When I asked my friend Glynnis Whitwer how she demonstrates grace in her parenting, she replied, "I learned to extend grace by allowing my kids to be who God designed them to be, not who I thought they should be. I have become a student of my children." Grace is in accepting and appreciating the natural talents and individual characteristics of our children. Trying to force a child to fit into our preferred mold will surely damage our relationship with them. Each child, by God's grace, has been given unique abilities. Paul confirms, "We have different gifts, according to the grace given us" (Romans 12:6a).

This verse spoke to me deeply concerning my daughter, Alex, who is bent toward generosity. She loves to give away her money and her toys. Recently, she worked diligently for weeks to earn a prize. When she finally won the big floppy hat that she had dreamed of and labored for, she gave it to her friend the next day.

When she told me it was her intention to give it away, I cautioned, "Alex, why would you want to give it away? You've been working to win that hat for weeks."

"I know," she replied, "but Ansley would really like it and I can't wait to see her face when I give it to her!"

At that moment, I realized that it would be a stumbling block to rob her of the joy of giving. I refocused my attention on encouraging her to glorify God with her generosity. To interfere with their God-given uniqueness by trying to alter their personalities, likes, or dislikes can hinder them from seeking God's will for their lives, thus hindering them from glorifying God with their gifts. Peter explained, "Each one should use whatever gift he has received to serve others, faithfully administering God's grace in its various forms" (1 Peter 4:10).

We are to encourage our children in their uniqueness. An elderly woman and her little grandson, whose face was sprinkled with bright freckles, spent the day at the zoo. Many children were waiting in line to get their cheeks painted by a local artist.

"You've got so many freckles, there's no place to paint!" a little girl in line said to the boy. Embarrassed, the little boy dropped his head.

His grandmother knelt down next to him. "I love your freckles. When I was a little girl I always wanted freckles," she said, while tracing her finger across the child's cheek. "Freckles are beautiful!"

The boy looked up. "Really?" he asked.

"Of course," said the grandmother. "Why, just name me one thing that's prettier than freckles."

The little boy thought for a moment, peered intensely into his grandma's face, and softly whispered, "Wrinkles."

When the grandma showed appreciation for the uniqueness of the child's freckles, he was encouraged to show appreciation back in a similar way. Appreciating and accepting others no matter how they look or act demonstrates God's grace. It is by the grace of God that we are who we are. Paul said in 1 Corinthians 15:10a, "But by the grace of God I am what I am."

Balance encouragement and correction. Pastor Al Jackson once said, "We have the opportunity to speak blessing or cursing into the lives of our children. We have the potential of bringing them to adulthood with a secure and stable sense of who they are. We also have the potential of bringing them to adulthood deeply scarred and wounded as a result of what we say or what we don't say."

If all we do is correct our children they will develop a distorted view of themselves and God. We should balance our corrections with encouragement so that they will have a healthy and sober assessment of themselves.

The greatest way to balance correction with encouragement is to use times of correction to encourage them in the hope of the gospel. Correction lends opportunity to point them to their need for Christ's grace and redemption. If we point out their sins without pointing them to the Savior, we have missed the purpose of discipline. To focus solely on wrong without offering the good news of the One who rights their wrongs, is to leave them without hope. Correction is the means we use to make them aware of their depravity, but it should also be the vehicle that drives them to redemption.

When Tommy yells at you in defiance he needs to be disciplined, but he also needs to be reminded of the hope that is his in Christ Jesus. Tommy needs to understand that he is not capable of being perfect all the time in his own strength, but through the transforming power of the Holy Spirit in his life, he is a new creation, holy and blameless before God.

A good indicator that the gospel is needed in the training process is seen in the child's response to correction. If Suzy becomes angry in the midst of correction, she is being prideful and denying the sinfulness of her heart. Anger says, "I do not deserve to be corrected and I refuse to accept instruction. I'm not so bad (regardless of what the Bible says). I wish my parents would just back off."

If Michael wallows in self-pity when corrected he is basing his worth on his own performance. Self-pity says, "My worth is based on how others view me (not on what Jesus has done for me). I am always messing up and in need of correction, therefore, I am worthless."

When Amy gets defensive and shifts blame elsewhere, she is showing a victim mentality. Defensiveness says, "I am being wrongly accused. Therefore, I must solicit sympathy by proving that I have done nothing wrong but fallen victim to injustice. It is up to me (not Jesus) to prove my righteousness."

Whether the child responds to correction by getting angry, indulging in self-pity, becoming defensive, or blame shifting, the heart issue is self-reliance. He is taking the responsibility for his justification out of God's hands and into his own. He is basing his righteousness on his own works and rejecting the work of Christ.

When we admonish our children for doing wrong but fail to point them to the grace of God for redemption, we communicate that righteousness is earned by doing good. By not encouraging them in the gospel, we fuel the fires of anger, self-pity, and defensiveness by causing them to rely on themselves. However, when we rebuke them for doing wrong while offering hope in Christ, we are teaching them to live freely as children of God. We are giving them a clear picture of themselves as sinking sinners and God as their rescuer.

We must teach them how the Word of God tells their own story and how living out the gospel means relying on the justification given to them (and us) through the death and resurrection of Jesus. The beauty of the gospel calls our children (and us) to confess their sinfulness while realizing that they are covered by grace, fully cleansed, fully forgiven, and fully clothed in the righteousness of Christ.

Pointing our children to God's grace as we teach, rebuke, correct, and train in the righteousness of Christ tells our children in a powerful way that God equates discipline with love. The Bible explains that God disciplines those he loves: "My son, do not despise the Lord's discipline and do not resent his rebuke, because the Lord disciplines those he loves, as a father the son he delights in" (Proverbs 3:11–12). Where there is no grace, only law and discipline, we risk our children viewing Christianity as nothing more than a legalistic religion. Paul said that we are not under law: "For sin shall not be your master, because you are not under law, but under grace" (Romans 6:14). Our homes will be filled with heavenly peace when the training of our children is grace-driven. May God be glorified as we acknowledge, accept, and apply his amazing grace in our parenting, and may our children be drawn to Christ!

Sixteen

Avoiding Traps of Ineffective Discipline

KING DAVID WAS CONSIDERED a man after God's own heart. He sinned big, repented big, and was a shining example to us all that God disciplines those he loves. However, King David did not, in turn, biblically discipline his own children. As a result, one son raped a half sister, another son, Absalom, murdered his brother in retaliation, and then led an armed rebellion against his own father, the king. Chapters 13 through 18 of 2 Samuel tell the tragic story of how a permissive King David failed to discipline Absalom after his murder of Amnon, his brother, and then the downward spiral to disaster as their family became embroiled in a hellish cycle of deceit, lies, betrayal, and finally death. While King David is a faithful example to us in many positive ways, he also gives testimony to the fact that failure to practice effective, biblical discipline can certainly destroy the peace and contentment that we desire for establishing heaven at home.

What about your home? Are you practicing ineffective methods of discipline, robbing your family of a peaceful home where relationships line up with God's Word? Do you find yourself threatening, repeating your instructions, or raising your voice in an attempt to get your children to obey? Are you frustrated because nothing seems to work? It could be that faulty child-training methods have snared your line of thinking. A quick bribe or mild threat appeals to a parent's appetite for gaining control of a child, especially in a hurried situation. So, we take the bait—hook, line, and sinker. It's not until later that we realize we're caught in a tangled net of ineffective parenting.

Remember that your goal is not merely to get children to obey outwardly, but to reach their hearts with the gospel of Christ. When we adopt faulty child-training methods that aim for behavior modification only, we miss the issues of the heart and the point of biblical discipline. Focusing on outward behavior runs the risk of transforming children into Pharisees by confusing children into believing that their acceptance is based on their own performance rather than God's grace. Paul said, "There is no one righteous, not even one" (Romans 3:10). In reality, our own righteous acts are like "filthy rags" (Isaiah 64:6). We are made righteous, not by our good behavior, but by the forgiveness and grace of God: "He saved us, not because of righteous things we had done, but because of his mercy. He saved us through the washing of rebirth and renewal by the Holy Spirit, whom he poured out on us generously through Jesus Christ our Savior, so that, having been justified by his grace, we might become heirs having the hope of eternal life" (Titus 3:5–7).

Certainly, God's law requires that children obey their parents outwardly. However, true obedience comes from a heart that desires to please God and respect God-given authority. Also, a child who obeys for the right reasons is a child that is truly happy. Have you ever noticed that the most content children are the ones that are trained in self-control and obedience? Children find security and peace in boundaries and standards. Therefore, children are happiest when they are safely kept under the protective umbrella of their parents' authority. Conversely, children who are allowed to be disobedient are not truly happy. In fact, they are rarely satisfied. True happiness is found only in a child whose heart delights in obeying God and his parents.

While many of the techniques parents are using to achieve obedience are popular, they are only good for temporary obedience, if they work at all. They may sound good, but anything that substitutes for God's ways will prove to be a snare in the end: "There is a way that seems right to a man, but in the end it leads to death" (Proverbs 14:12). We must be on guard against the pitfalls of pop psychology, lest we become entrapped in the snares of ineffective parenting.

Ineffective Parenting

Time-Out. Of all the latest methods, "time-out" seems to be the most popular. Time-out is actually quite humorous if you think about it. I've had many frazzled moms call me because they can't get their child to sit during "time-out." Mom puts the child in the time-out chair and he gets up. Mom puts him back in the time-out chair and he gets up again. After so many rounds of "tag, you're it," Mom is so upset and defeated that she doesn't even remember why the child was put in time-out to begin with! While these techniques are supposed to be based on the brilliance of modern child psychology, they have made discipline much harder than it has to be. You don't put a jewel thief in an unsupervised jewelry store to train him not to steal; you don't put an alcoholic in a liquor store for rehabilitation; and you don't put a child who lacks self-control in a time-out chair and expect him to be still. We must be careful not to lead our children into temptation. Our goal is to encourage them in righteousness for the glory of God.

Time-out opens the door for a power struggle. God's way is much easier and much more effective. If a child disobeys, is it not easier to spank the child and be done with it than to enter the power struggle of time-out? Not only can time-out be extremely exasperating to a child, but it also gives him the upper hand in determining the effectiveness of the consequence. After all, he is the one who will determine whether or not he actually sits or gets up. To spank a child is to heed the command of God for training the child in wisdom, keeping the upper hand as a parent in control of the consequence, and avoiding the endless atrocity of an unnecessary battle of the wills. A wise parent understands, "The rod of correction imparts wisdom, but a child left to himself disgraces his mother" (Proverbs 29:15).

Time-out leaves the child to himself. Time-out replaces "time in" with Mom and the working of the Holy Spirit through her obedience to God's Word in discipline. When Mom leaves the child to himself in time-out rather than interacting with him, teaching him the word of God, and lovingly correcting him with the rod, she disregards God's intention for her to play an active role in the training of her child. She also puts her child in danger. According to Proverbs 23:13–14, failure to punish with the rod places the child at risk: "Do not withhold discipline from a child; if you punish him with the rod, he will not die. Punish him with the rod and save his soul from death."

Bribing. To bribe a child into obeying is to motivate him wrongly. Bribing encourages children in selfishness, as their motive for obeying is personal gain. Bribing sounds like, "If you clean your room you can rent a movie tonight" or "If you don't misbehave in the grocery store, you can pick out candy at the checkout counter." Children should be taught to obey because it is right and because it pleases God, not to get a reward. The Bible says, "Children, obey your parents in everything, for this pleases the Lord" (Colossians 3:20). We should simply state the standard and follow through with consequences when that standard is violated.

Counting to Three. As we train our children to obey us we are ultimately training them to obey Jesus. Do we want our children to obey God the first time, the second time, or the third time? When we count to three, we allow our children to get into the habit of delayed obedience. Delayed obedience is disobedience. Counting to three encourages them to put off obeying until absolutely necessary.

We want our children to view obedience as their only option, not a choice that is put off until the last minute.

Threatening. This is one of my biggest struggles in parenting. I'm so tempted to say, "If you don't do this, then this will be the consequences." Moms, this is how we get ourselves in a pickle. If we tell them there will be a consequence then, by golly, there better be one. Otherwise, we might cause them to question our word. A woman of integrity says what she means and means what she says. If we cry wolf too many times, we will eventually lose our effectiveness as well as the respect of our children. Our children need to have confidence that our word is our word.

Appealing to their emotions. Allow me to brag about my son for a minute. Wesley is an extraordinary eleven-year-old boy. He considers my feelings and needs above his own. This is a child who listens for me to arrive home from grocery shopping so that he can rush out and insist on bringing in the groceries. If I'm going out in the rain, he reminds me to get an umbrella. He refuses to leave the kitchen after dinner before he has helped me clear the table. He brings me breakfast in bed when I'm sick, cleans my bathroom each week, and if I'm having a bad day he'll ask, "Mom, is there something I can do for you?" I'm telling you, the child is one of a kind.

I recently caught myself taking advantage of his others-oriented bent by playing on his emotions. He had been outside playing with his sister for a couple of hours, while I was busy cleaning the windows and blinds. He came in and asked if I would ride bikes around the block with them. I replied with all the exasperation I could muster, "Somebody's got to clean the windows and blinds. Then I have to cook supper and answer emails." I adjusted the chip clip that was holding my disheveled hair and added in my most *please feel sorry for me voice*, "I'd also like to vacuum before Dad gets home, but with everything else I have to do around here, I doubt I'll have time for that." I even dropped the Windex bottle as I stomped by for dramatic effect. While I achieved the results I was after, God pierced my heart with Wesley's selfless response, "I'll vacuum for you, Mom. I don't mind helping out." Oh, the guilt. I immediately asked his forgiveness for manipulating him, rather than simply asking for his help. Then I let him vacuum!

Other ways of appealing to their emotions might include giving them the silent treatment or the cold shoulder. Manipulative statements might sound like, "After all I do for you, this is how you show your appreciation!" or "If you cared about me, you would do what I say." We should not manipulate our children by playing on their emotions. We do not want them to become pleasers of man, but pleasers of God. Therefore, we should not dangle their love for us as bait in order to enforce an emotional response. Instead, we should encourage our children to obey for the glory of God.

Reasoning with small children. Parents should avoid trying to talk their children into obedience. Reasoning with small children erases the line of authority between the parent and the child, and may place the parent in a position of being outsmarted! Here's a scenario of a reasoning parent:

Mom: "Oh, Sweetheart, you probably need to color with markers on the floor instead of on the couch."

Child: "I'm being careful, Mom."

Mom: "But you might accidentally get marker on the couch."

Child: "I don't think I will because I'm holding my paper in my lap."

Mom: "But it would be safer to color on the floor."

Rather than simply instructing her child to get on the floor with his markers, the mom is trying to talk him into obedience by reasoning with him. We should avoid statements like, "Are you ready to go to bed?" and "Don't you think you should brush your teeth?"

and "Why don't we pick up the toys before lunch?" Asking the child if he would like to do something places him on a peer level with the parent. The parent who tries to reason with her child usually ends up frustrated, and the child usually ends up disrespecting her authority by arguing rather than obeying. Sometimes I wonder if it might be beneficial for us to play a recording of "I am the parent, I am the parent, I am the parent" over and over in order to brainwash us into acting like it!

Manipulating their environment. Mom is talking on the phone. Little Jenny grabs the remote control from the coffee table. As Mom continues talking, she takes the remote control from Jenny and places it on top of the mantle. Jenny wobbles over to the end table and pulls the picture frame off. It crashes onto the hardwood floor and the glass shatters. As Mom is collecting the broken glass, Jenny has already found another picture frame on the other end table. Mom puts her friend on hold as she yells, "Jenny, put that back!" Jenny puts it back, waits for Mom to resume talking, and grabs it again. Mom snatches the frame from Jenny and places it on the mantle. As Mom rearranges the accessories in the living room, Jenny looks for something that Mom can't move.

Mom has taught Jenny that if something is within her reach, it's okay for her to grab it. She has taught her that the only things that are off limits are the things that are not within her reach. Mom has manipulated Jenny's environment rather than taking the opportunity to train her in self-control and obedience. We are provided with natural opportunities to train our children to obey. We should seize opportunities to train our children in the ways of the Lord rather than avoiding discipline by manipulating the situation.

When are they old enough to learn to obey? When they're old enough to disobey. Training to obey typically starts once they can crawl and "get into" things. Crawlers can easily learn not to touch certain items if they are trained in one room at a time, rather than having free reign of the whole house. Training them what's off limits in one room at a time prevents exasperating them with too much training at one time. Peace comes through boundaries.

Repeating or going back on instructions. In studying some of the most admirable and successful generals of our country, I have found that they all had one thing in common: they were certain of their commands before they issued them. Soldiers do not respect or respond well to an uncertain and inconsistent leader. Paul said it best in 1 Corinthians 14:8, "For if the trumpet makes an uncertain sound, who will prepare for battle?" (NKJV). Likewise, when Mom issues half-hearted commands to her children and doesn't require her children to follow through immediately, she sends them mixed signals. Not only will this sort of leadership earn Mom the "most wishy-washy in command" medal, but her children will become uncertain of when and how to respond to Mom's instructions. However, when we lead our "troops" with confidence, they find security and stability in their call to obedience.

We should never issue a warning or command without following it through. This rule of thumb requires that we think before we speak. In Matthew we are told, "Simply let your 'Yes' be 'Yes,' and your 'No,' 'No'; anything beyond this comes from the evil one" (Matthew 5:37). We should try not to say "yes" or "no" to something until we are sure that it is our definite answer. According to Proverbs 15:28, it is biblical that we think before speaking: "The heart of the righteous *weighs* its answers." Let us weigh our answers, give confident commands, and raise up a mighty army for the Lord!

Effective Parenting

The first step toward effective parenting is to realize that biblical obedience is complete, immediate, and evinced with joy. You might teach this concept to younger children by explaining that obedience is all the way, right away, and with a joyful heart.

The second step toward effective parenting is to expect nothing less than biblical obedience. Don't be wishy-washy or you'll raise wishy-washy children who have a hard time determining when to and when not to submit to authority. Determine the "family rules" and establish a strong family identity in Christ by expecting your children to obey authority.

The third step toward effective parenting is to administer consequences faithfully when children are disobedient. To disobey authority is to live foolishly. It is the parent's responsibility to administer the rod, which God uses to drive foolishness from the hearts of children: "Folly is bound up in the heart of a child, but the rod of discipline will drive it far from him" (Proverbs 22:15). There are two areas of foolishness (folly) that need correcting:

Direct disobedience. When a child is given a command, understands that command, and willfully disregards that command, he is being directly disobedient. One way to proactively encourage our children to obey is to talk about obedience in times of non-conflict. For example, if your family is on the way to have dinner with friends, you might go over what's expected before you arrive. Rather than rattling off a list of rules, you might ask, "What are some ways that you can please God while we are at Mr. and Mrs. Martin's house?" If you are traveling to the grocery store, consider asking, "Who can name three ways to obey Mom in the grocery store?" Simply reviewing what's expected beforehand establishes accountability in a non-threatening way and encourages the children in righteousness. Don't forget to compliment obedient behavior on the ride home!

Defiant attitude. When a child expresses rebellion with his body language, words, or tone of voice, he is not obeying. The Lord has commanded that all of his children, young and old, obey with a joyful heart: "Do everything without complaining or arguing" (Philippians

2:14). Keep in mind that having a right attitude is a choice. Children are acting on their emotions when they respond with a bad attitude. While emotions are good, we don't want our children to become enslaved by their emotions. I often remind my children, "You are choosing to have a bad attitude. It would be better to stop, get a hold on your emotions, and purpose in your heart to glorify Christ with your attitude."

While I am not an advocate of "time-out," I do believe that a "reflective time-out" can be beneficial. A reflective time-out is not a consequence for disobedience, but takes place before the spark becomes a fire. When my children start in with a bad attitude, I'll often hold up both hands and say, "Stop. Go take a few minutes and think before you say anything else. Consider how you might respond with wisdom before you get in trouble." This isn't to say that children may not discuss their feelings with us or ask questions. Children should have much freedom to express themselves openly and honestly, but this should be done with self-control and respect.

By avoiding the snares of ineffective parenting and adhering to God's design for discipline, we move past the frustrations of not knowing how to handle issues of disobedience and into a confident, well-balanced approach to raising our children.

PART FIVE

Home is Heavenly

When it Serves as a Haven

Seventeen

Structuring Your Day Brings Peace to Your Home

PLANNING A ROUTINE in accordance with our priorities enables us to better fulfill our God-given responsibilities. Personally, when I don't adhere to a well-thought-out plan, I find that I lose focus on my priorities and I become frustrated and overwhelmed. I get wrapped up in the moment and lose sight of what is really important. I am selfish by nature and it shows when I don't set goals to meet the responsibilities that God has laid out for me in his Word.

As women of many hats, we are wise to think through and write down a regular schedule to follow throughout the week so that our daily habits prove to be beneficial and good for the whole family. Without a structured routine, our good intentions will remain just that. Routine allows us to meet the needs of our family in an orderly fashion, which brings a rewarding sense of accomplishment and confidence in our roles as wives and moms. We are good stewards when our time is spent wisely. Here are a few benefits to having a routine:

Routine enables us to avoid idleness. Proverbs 31 describes a woman of noble character. In verse 27 we are told, "She watches over the affairs of her household and does not eat the bread of idleness." It is an unwise use of time to busy ourselves with things that cater to our momentary wants, while remaining idle in taking care of the affairs of the household. We must learn to balance our wants with our responsibilities for the sake of glorifying God and for the good of our families. Paul warned women against the dangers of going from one thing to the next without reason: "Besides, they get into the habit of being idle and going about from house to house. And not only do they become idlers, but also gossips and busybodies, saying things they ought not to" (1 Timothy 5:13).

Every year, I look forward to vacation. I dream of lying on the beach, napping in the breeze, reading a good fiction book, and doing absolutely nothing. Each vacation, I enjoy doing exactly that . . . for about three days. Then I begin to go stark-raving mad. God did not design us to be idle. We are told that working is part of God's plan for us: "Whatever you do, work at it with all your heart, as working for the Lord, not for men, since you know that you will receive an inheritance from the Lord as a reward. It is the Lord Christ you are serving" (Colossians 3:23–24). He designed us to work diligently for his glory.

Because accountability is minimal for women who stay home, I believe it is easier for the full-time homemaker to fall into a pattern of laziness. Therefore, we must remember that although we do not serve a boss who fires us for not performing to his expectations or rewards us with a raise when we exceed them, we do serve the God of the universe who delights in our obedience.

We are told in Proverbs to consider the ant as an example of God's plan for work: "Go to the ant, you sluggard, consider its ways and be wise. It has no commander, no overseer or ruler, yet it stores its provisions in summer and gathers its food at harvest. How long will you lie there, you sluggard? A little sleep, a little slumber, a little folding of the hands to rest—and poverty will come on you like a bandit and scarcity like an armed man" (Proverbs 6:6–11). Idleness results in laziness, unbalance, unfruitfulness, and ingratitude for a God who blesses us as we work for his glory. A woman of noble character is described as a woman who "works with eager hands" (Proverbs 31:13) and "sets about her work vigorously" (Proverbs 31:17).

God commands us to not be idle. If you struggle with idleness, Paul's words may help, "Whatever you do, do your work heartily, as for the Lord rather than for men, knowing that from the Lord you will receive the reward of the inheritance. It is the Lord Christ whom you serve" (Colossians 3:23–25, NASB). With his help, you can overcome idleness, and by his grace, he forgives you when you fail.

His grace is often abused in the flippant way we view sin. We know he'll forgive us, so we do as we please with the intention to repent later. However, when we fully grasp his atonement as the gift it is, we no longer view disobedience as no big deal. We recognize the *sin now, repent later* mentality as the poison that separates us from God. Therefore, we aim to keep his commands by holding to Jesus, in obedience and disobedience, in order that we might glorify him in all that we do.

Routine enables us to have more freedom. When we operate under a routine, we actually have more free time. Taking the *whatever comes my way* approach to accomplishing things leads to an *I'm never caught up* sense of frustration. With this work ethic, we find ourselves running from one thing to the next without ever feeling the satisfaction of being on top of things. We become enslaved to unfinished chores that scream for our attention, rob us of real freedom, and mentally zap our strength. Freedom comes with establishing a reasonable plan of action for each day. Having a starting point as well as an attainable finish line gives us incentive for winning the race of responsibility. Also, free time is more enjoyable without other responsibilities looming over our heads. Setting realistic goals and working diligently to accomplish those goals enables us to enjoy the down times more fully.

While free time is needed, too much of it can lead to sin. Television can be a relaxing way to unwind, but unlimited freedom in watching television can lead to impure thoughts and lack of contentment. Talking on the telephone with friends can be enjoyable, but unlimited freedom in talking on the telephone can lead to gossip and slander. Shopping can be fun, but unlimited freedom in shopping can lead to poor stewardship and disharmony in the marriage. Letting household chores go for a good reason can bring balance, but unlimited freedom in completing household chores can lead to laziness. While free time is good for us, too much freedom in anything can lead to bondage.

Routine enables us to avoid unnecessary stress. Some stress is beneficial as it provides the occasions to develop character, produce spiritual growth, and rely more fully on Christ. However, it is unnecessary to feel stress as a result of being unorganized and/or lazy. We want to avoid the stress and chaos that come from running from one thing to the next on a daily basis. An undisciplined life hinders us from accomplishing necessary tasks that minister to the needs of our families.

While stress results from an undisciplined and unstructured home life, it can also be a result of *too much* discipline and structure. If you are a structured person and your family members seem stressed out, consider whether your desire to adhere to a routine is too rigid. If cleaning the house and following your schedule takes precedence over your relationship with God, your husband, or your children, then you have gone too far the other way. While a schedule is helpful for keeping order, freedom comes with flexibility. Don't become a slave to your schedule. The ability to let some things slide, when necessary, brings balance to your routine.

Consider the uniqueness of your family

This chapter, as well as the next two, will offer simple tips for creating a structured routine. Please do not feel that if you are not following these tips you are a bad wife and/or mom. You may have a wonderful routine that works well for your family. These chapters are written for those who are frustrated with their daily routine and searching for help to create order out of chaos. As you read through these ideas, consider which ones might improve your homemaking, and forget about the ones that won't.

All families are different. I dare say that no one routine is just right for all families. You must assess the needs of your individual family and organize your routine accordingly. Resist the temptation to compare yourself to others who seem more organized, but it is good to glean ideas that might help you.

Trying to pattern your schedule after another woman's can be a dangerous endeavor. "Measuring up" to others is not your goal. When someone else's organizational abilities become the measuring stick we use to judge our own abilities, we will battle either pride or despair. We will either measure up or not. However, our confidence does not come from being as good as someone else, but by trusting in Christ to be all that we are not.

My hope is to be like him and to glorify him. He has made me who I am. He loves me regardless of my shortcomings. He doesn't look at me and say, "You're not as good as Linda because you aren't organized." He looks at me and says, "I created you with strengths to fulfill my purpose for you, and weaknesses that my strength would be glorified through you." Therefore, I will not envy another's ability and strength, but will cling to my Lord who gives me his ability and strength.

Although I fall, I will not wallow in hopelessness, for my Jesus lifts me up and faithfully carries me over the sea of my iniquities. Why should I want to be like anyone but Jesus? He is my role model and he has lovingly made me in his own image. I will not look to the left or right, but to the One who covers my inadequacies with his perfection.

God has plans for me that are different from his plans for others, just as he had specific plans for his people in the book of Jeremiah.

"For I know the plans I have for you," declares the Lord, "plans to prosper you and not to harm you, plans to give you hope and a future" (Jeremiah 29:11). That prophecy was written to Israelites who had been captured and taken away from the Promised Land and away from the Temple where God had dwelled among them for centuries. But even in exile, God's people were not on their own. Today as well, God has plans for his people. It boggles my mind and warms my heart to know that God has custom-designed my family for his glory.

Consider Your Priorities

We organize a routine based on our priorities. If our priorities are to be a growing child of God, a wife of noble character, and a godly mother, then we must plan our days to reflect those priorities.

A growing child of God. We are children of God who must put aside time to nurture our relationships with him. While there are some seasons when it is not possible to spend time in God's Word in the mornings, it is best to begin our day with him when we can. We know from Mark 1:35 that Jesus met with the Father first thing in the morning: "Very early in the morning while it was still dark, Jesus got up, left his house and went off to a solitary place, where he prayed." Because it was still dark, Jesus' disciples were probably still sleeping. We also see that Jesus chose a solitary place where he would not be interrupted. I don't know about you, but the only time I will not be interrupted is while my children are sleeping. In addition to my children's needs, once the day gets going, distractions such as the telephone, email, errands, school, and a slew of other responsibilities demand my attention and pull me away from uninterrupted time with Jesus.

*A **wife** of **noble** character.* There was once a woman who was married to a miserly man. She wanted to go shopping one day, but she knew that her husband wouldn't like it as he didn't like her to spend money. She pleaded with her husband to let her go and she assured him that it was just for fun. She promised that she would only window shop and she wouldn't buy anything. On her way out the door, her husband warned, "Remember, you better not buy anything!" A few hours later the wife came home wearing a brand new dress. The husband was furious and demanded an explanation. So the wife gave him one.

"Well," she said, "I thought the dress was so cute on the mannequin. I didn't think it would hurt anything to try it on. It was never my intention to buy it, but when I put it on, the devil said, 'It sure does look good on you!'"

"Right!" the husband replied, "That's when you should have said, 'Get thee behind me, Satan!'"

"That's exactly what I said!" the wife yelled, "But when he got behind me he said, 'Oh, Honey, it looks even better from the back!'"

A godly wife brings good to her husband: "She brings him good, not harm, all the days of her life" (Proverbs 31:12). One way that we bring good to our husbands is by spending the family income wisely. The Proverbs 31 woman did not spend money on frivolous items. Actually, she saved money and figured out ways to make it grow: "She considers a field and buys it; out of her earnings she plants a vineyard" (Proverbs 31:16). Rather than spending every dime that was hers to spend, she put some aside until she had enough to purchase a worthy investment.

We also learn from Proverbs that her husband had full confidence in her. He did not have to check up on her spending, suspend her credit cards, or monitor her checkbook. She had proven herself worthy in managing the family's money wisely, not selfishly. The Scriptures indicate that her husband profited from her money-managing skills: "Her husband has full confidence in her and lacks nothing of value" (Proverbs 31:11). In other words, he is not poor (he lacks nothing of value) because of her foolishly spending his earnings.

A godly mother. A godly mother is available to nurture and train her children. Moms can better meet the needs of their children if there is not chaos during the day. Having structure and routine enables Mom to be more readily available when she is needed. If we have no order to our days, then our time will be given to things other than our families. One time-robbing culprit is the telephone. If you are irritated by your children's constant interruptions while you are on the telephone, it could be an indicator that you are more available to callers than to your children. Certainly, children should be taught to respect Mom's time on the telephone, but we must be careful not to exasperate them by always being on the telephone. If the telephone dictates our time, we can become tangled in a web of a disorderly home. A mom who structures her day will return calls at convenient times, rather than dropping everything to chat. Consider good times to talk, such as while small children are napping or having a scheduled playtime, and plan your conversations during those times. An answering machine is a godsend. Use it to screen calls and to postpone talking until a more convenient time.

I've been guilty of letting email consume too much of my time. My computer is in our schoolroom. I used to keep my computer online at all times to ensure that I could hear incoming emails. Big mistake. The "ding" of an email would draw me away from a math lesson quicker than Garfield is drawn to the sound of the can opener. Of course, my intentions would always be to read it quickly and respond after school. But then I would think, *Well, it'll only take a minute to respond.* Twenty minutes later, my type C personality child is frustrated by my whimsical indulgence, and my type A personality child has closed her book, grabbed a coke, and headed outside. We all wind up frustrated and irritable when 2:00 rolls around and school has yet to be finished. My solution? I keep my computer offline until school assignments are completed.

God always provides a way to overcome temptation: "No temptation has seized you except what is common to man. And God is faithful; he will not let you be tempted beyond what you can bear. But when you are tempted, he will also provide a way out so that you can stand up under it" (1 Corinthians 10:13). If you're home schooling, cleaning house, preparing a meal, sharing a meal, or expecting your husband home at any minute, consider letting callers leave voice messages and cyber-friends wait until a better time for your reply. When I choose not to check email or answer the telephone while I am interacting with my family, I am less likely to be lured away by time-robbing temptations. Also, letting callers leave messages sends your children a powerful message that they are of vital importance to you.

Be a Calendar Girl

If my house were to catch fire and I could only salvage two things (not counting my family and our family photos, of course), I would most definitely grab my Bible and my calendar. My whole life is written on my calendar. Every appointment, every meal, and everything else that happens between sunrise and sunset is penned in that one place. If it ain't on my calendar, it ain't gonna happen, because I ain't gonna remember it.

Recording appointments on your calendar as soon as they are made can keep you from missing them and cut down on the clutter of sticky-notes or piles of papers. If everything else is written on your calendar as well, it can prevent you from having to reschedule appointments because of previous, forgotten commitments. Choosing a calendar with every day of the month on one page will help you prepare for birthdays, upcoming events, and meals. If you only check one day at a time (a one day per page calendar), you might find yourself rushing around to make last minute preparations.

My calendar aids me in planning meals, which keeps my grocery bill down. I double recipes when I prepare dinner, ensuring leftovers for another night. Consider cooking two nights in a row, then rotating the leftovers so that the same meal isn't served back to back. This way you have two nights on and two nights off. If money allows, consider budgeting a "dine out" one night each week, or every other week. This allows a fun family outing with no clean up! Remember, the Proverbs 31 woman saved her money to spend on wise investments. Rather than purchasing unneeded and unhealthy junk food, save that money for your family's night out. Put it in an envelope and tuck it away, lest you be tempted to spend it on something else.

I must say that keeping a calendar as I have suggested is not a biblical mandate. If my ideas encourage and help you to instill desired order into your routine, then go for it. However, if they are not for you, that's okay too. If need be, take them with a grain of salt and move on.

Keep an Add-To-It List

An add-to-it list can keep you from making too many trips to the store, which typically results in over-spending. When you put that last roll of toilet paper in the bathroom, add that item to your list immediately. As soon as you notice the toothpaste getting low, add it to the list. I like to keep one extra of items that I do not want to run out of, such as toilet paper, cleaning supplies, laundry detergent, and toothpaste. When the toothpaste gets low and I add it to the list, I actually have a spare so that I don't have to make an emergency trip to the store if it runs out before my shopping day. When we make frequent trips to the store for such items as these, we typically come out with more than we went in for. Having a "back up" of the important stuff keeps us from making extra trips to the store. If you can't afford to purchase an extra of the necessities, consider adding one extra item to your list each week, until you build your "back up" supply. The time and money saved will be well worth it.

Before making your weekly or bi-weekly trip to the grocery store, plan your meals for the week(s). Check to see which ingredients you already have, jotting down the ones you will need. If you have kept a good add-to-it list all week, you should only have to add items for meal preparation before you venture off to shop. Having a list of what's needed saves time and money, enabling us to be good stewards of both.

"No" is the Magic Word

"No" just might be the single most powerful word for maintaining a balanced life. Women who say "yes" to every opportunity to serve find themselves frustrated and overwhelmed by the everyday chores of life. Often, we say "yes" because we don't want to disappoint others or we desire their praise. However, John tells us to love praise from God, not from men (John 12:43). We should be more concerned with pleasing God and seeking his will for our lives. We can be sure that it is not his will that we walk past our families in order to minister to others.

Other times, it is our inability to relinquish control that causes us to overcommit. To commit to something simply because we feel it will only be done right if we are involved is an issue of control. This need for control not only causes us to serve where we are not called to serve, but also hinders someone else from serving where they are supposed to serve. Control can keep us, as well as others, from following the path of God.

When we think that we must be involved in every planning session, every event, every committee, and every service opportunity to ensure success, we are judging the abilities of others and thinking of ourselves more highly than we should. Paul warns, "Therefore, let us stop passing judgment on one another. Instead, make up your mind not to put any stumbling block or obstacle in your brother's way" (Romans 14:13). We become stumbling blocks to others when we take an area of service that God meant for someone else.

In order to avoid saying "yes" to the wrong things, it might be wise to wait before responding to an invitation to serve by saying, "Let me get back with you on that." We can guard against overcommitting by seeking God's will before answering. It's wise to talk it over with our husbands before making a commitment. We should also consider whether or not a particular area of service lines up with our gifts and talents. In Proverbs we are told to think before we give an answer: "The heart of the righteous weighs its answers, but the mouth of the wicked gushes evil" (Proverbs 15:28). There is wisdom in carefully considering what we should and should not do. Paul admonishes us, "Be very careful, then, how you live—not as unwise but as wise, making the most of every opportunity, because the days are evil. Therefore do not be foolish, but understand what the Lord's will is" (Ephesians 4:15–17).

Jesus didn't say "yes" to every opportunity to heal people, nor did he sit and visit with everyone he came in contact with. How did he choose which areas of ministry to pursue and which ones to turn down? He asked his Father in Heaven and set his agenda accordingly. It was after Jesus prayed all night that God revealed who his twelve disciples would be. When we seek God's direction in his word and pray for God's guidance, he gives us wisdom and insight. When we walk in his will for our lives, we enjoy his peace.

Plan to Rest on Sunday

The Bible says, "For six days work is to be done, but the seventh day is a Sabbath of rest, holy to the Lord" (Exodus 31:15a). If Sundays find you rushing around, arguing with your spouse and children, and irritable, you may need to re-evaluate your priorities for this day on which God commands us to rest. God tells us to rest on Sunday because he knows we *need* to rest on Sunday. Whether or not you obey God's command for the Sabbath can greatly affect your attitude the rest of the week.

Preparation for rest on Sunday begins on Monday. If weekly responsibilities are met Monday—Saturday, then a restful Sunday is more attainable and certainly more enjoyable. Make a few extra preparations on Saturday to ensure an easy-going Sabbath. Prepare your meal for Sunday dinner on Saturday, have your table set before you go to bed, set out what everyone will wear, and have your Bibles and other items for church gathered and ready. Go to bed at a reasonable hour Saturday night and get up in plenty of time Sunday morning. There is nothing peaceful about rushing around in a tizzy trying to make it to church on time. Strive for a peaceful morning by being prepared and rested.

Avoid household chores and running errands on Sunday. Instead, play games or ride bikes together, take a nap, slide into a candlelit bubble bath, or snuggle on the couch with a cozy blanket and a good book. Beware of allowing "good" church activities to rob your family of resting on the Sabbath. The good is an enemy to the best. What's best is to obey God.

God commands that the Sabbath be set apart for worship and rest, but we must be careful not to judge others in how they "rest." We shouldn't think that the way we have chosen to honor the Sabbath is the only right way. Celebrating the Sabbath is mandatory; the method is not. Methods will look different for each family and probably for each season. We must not judge someone who doesn't keep "our law."

We must be careful not to confuse our personal choices concerning Sabbath keeping with biblical truth. Truth is that we are commanded to rest on the Sabbath, but how we specifically keep that command is not given. I've mentioned ideas for preparing to rest on Sundays, but my ideas mustn't be equated with God's commands.

By seeking to please Jesus in all that we do, being good stewards of our time, making plans to adequately accomplish our responsibilities as wives and moms, and scheduling a routine that best enables us to meet the needs of our families, we glorify God and create a heavenly home of order and peace.

Eighteen

Structuring Your Child's Day
Brings Peace to Your Home

CHILDREN WITH LITTLE OR NO STRUCTURE tend to be whiney, bored, unmotivated, irresponsible, and discontent. Lack of structure can also lead to behavioral problems such as tantrums, arguing, demanding language, and inability to focus and follow through on instructions. A wise mom will build structure and routine into her child's day for the purpose of building his character and keeping peace in the home. Certainly, every minute of every day does not have to be structured, but when a basic plan of action is set, children learn that order is a prerequisite for good living.

If your child has not been benefiting from an orderly life, consider adding some of the following ideas to his daily routine. Please keep in mind that these are merely ideas and suggestions, not biblical mandates. If you struggle with structure, don't be discouraged. A wise mother knows her worth is in Christ, not in her own efforts. She remembers that the God who created the stars and calls them all by name (Isaiah 40:26) is the God of order, and he has ordered all the days of her life. She depends on Christ to be all that she is not.

Ideas for Infants

Nap Time—Naps are necessary for a baby's well-being. Obviously, an infant is not capable of scheduling adequate naptimes. Mom should schedule her infant's naps in accordance with what's best for him, not what he wants. It's a good idea to develop an organized feed/wake/sleep routine. Rather than feeding your baby and then immediately putting him down for a nap, consider allowing his wake time to be while he is full and content. This way, he is more likely to sleep until the next feeding time. For example, if your six-week-old is on a three-hour feeding schedule, he would eat and have "wake time" for the first hour then sleep for the next two. Babies tend to be more content just after eating; therefore, planning their wake time while they are full and their naptime while they are building their hunger back up, leads to a more peaceful routine for you and your baby. Of course, as they grow older, the routine would allow for more wake time, less sleep time, and longer stretches between feedings.

Playpen Time—Get your baby used to spending time in a playpen. Rotate him from his tummy to his back, which will protect him from becoming sore from the same position. Attach an activity center that lights up and plays music for him to look at.

Blanket Time—Crib gyms with toys that dangle over your baby stimulate his focusing skills. Time on a blanket allows a change in environment.

Bouncy-Seat or Car-Seat Time—Place the seat by a window or in the kitchen while you cook. Again, this simply changes your baby's position and environment.

Swing Time—Swings are fun and offer your baby variety but be careful not to use your swing as a tool to get him to sleep as this can result in a habit that is hard to break. There are always exceptions to the rule, but overall, it's best to teach babies to fall asleep on their own, without props. Therefore, consider using the swing when he is awake and alert.

Bath Time—It's sometimes helpful to plan your baby's bath during his fussy time of the day. Warm water sponged over a fussy baby can be soothing. Sing and talk to your baby during this time, as they love to hear the comforting voice of Mom.

Interaction Time—While there's not a lot you can do to actually play with an infant, remember that just talking, cuddling, and moving his arms and legs in a playful manner express attention and love. Begin reading to your children at a young age, even when they can't comprehend the words. This increases their attention span and establishes an early appreciation for reading.

Errands—Running errands together serves as an exciting outing for a baby. Try to schedule errands after your baby has had a nap and a meal. When possible, plan on returning home in time for the next nap to keep your baby on a steady routine of proper rest.

Ideas for Toddlers

Playpen Time—Playpen time teaches toddlers to play alone contentedly, increases attention span, and develops focusing skills. Allow only two or three toys so that your toddler is not overwhelmed. If you are just now incorporating playpen time, serve Cheerios and a bottle or cup of juice to ensure that it gets off to a good start. Begin with 5–10 minutes a day, working up to the time you want. For toddlers who are accustomed to playpen time you might schedule 30–60 minutes once or twice a day. Keep a basket in the corner of the playpen and help your toddler learn to put his toys away when playpen time is over. Playpen time assures you that your child is in a safe environment while you complete other tasks. It can also serve as a familiar place for Baby to sleep when the family is traveling.

Blanket Time—This is great for teaching self-control, obedience, and the importance of boundaries. Again, provide a few toys and require the toddler to stay on the blanket. Our family enjoyed a cabin on the lake when my daughter was eighteen months old. Because she was trained to blanket time, she was able to enjoy being out on the pier with the family for long periods of time. Blanket time can also be beneficial while you are getting your hair cut or waiting for an appointment and need your toddler to play alone with self-control.

High Chair or Booster Chair Time—Provide a coloring book or puzzle. Set the timer and have the child play quietly until the timer goes off. Again, this not only brings structure to your child's day, but also teaches him self-control, obedience, contentment, and focusing skills.

Computer Time—There are many fun computer games for toddlers that are rich in creative and learning activities.

Reading and Prayer Time—Bedtime is a great time to sit with your child in your lap and read to him. List things you are thankful for and teach him to pray, "Thank you, God, for. . . ." Having Mom's undivided attention warming his heart and thoughts of a loving God who provides for him is a wonderful way to end the day and drift off to dreamland.

Video Time—Videos provide monitored entertainment for the child as well as free time for Mom. Have a set amount of time for video viewing so that it is a beneficial tool, not a babysitter. Avoid videos that contain scary images that can play on the child's mind and cause bad dreams, too much action that can make him hyper or nervous, and smart-alecky role models that can influence his character in negative ways. Remember, what's down in the well comes up in the bucket!

Outside Time—Plan time outside each day. Fresh air and plenty of running space are good for the mind and body—yours and your toddler's.

Ideas for Preschool-aged children

Room Time—Consider switching from playpen time to room time between the ages of 20–24 months. Having playpen time in the child's room for a month or so, allows him to adjust to being alone in his room and prepares him for the switch. Room time promotes creativity and imagination if you allow only a few toys or activities to be out at one time. Too many toys will hinder a child from focusing. Rotate room time toys every few days for variety. Room time can enhance the sibling relationship by simply allowing time apart. It also allows Mom time to prepare meals, return phone calls, start the laundry, etc. My children often enjoyed books on tape during room time. Use a timer to avoid the question, "How much longer?" You might also consider using a gate at the door until your child is accustomed to room time. Be cheerful when you announce that it is room time. Don't wait until the children are getting on your nerves and present it as a way to get away from them for an hour or they will view it as punishment. Let it simply be a part of their day that is meant for their enjoyment.

Sit Time—As your child moves from the toddler years, replace high-chair time or booster-chair time with sit time. Have the child sit in a chair or on the couch with a book or activity. Children who are accustomed to high-chair time will transition well to sit time. Again, this is a time to be quiet and focus on the task at hand. A timer is helpful here as well. Sit time is beneficial for teaching children to sit in church. Waiting until children start attending "big church" to train them to sit quietly is disrespectful to others. Sit time is an effective way for preparing your child for a smooth transition from nursery to "big church," making the move more pleasant for the child, the parent, the pastor, and the congregation.

Other Activities—Of course, scheduling computer activities, television, videos, and outside play is as appropriate for older children as younger. Scheduling and monitoring these activities (especially computer and television) keeps children from overdosing on a good thing. Studies show that spending excessive amounts of time playing computer games and watching television stunts vocabulary and creativity.

Chores—Assigned chores can start as early as two years old. A two-year-old can put his toys away, clear his plate and cup from the table, undress himself and put his clothes in a hamper. A three-year-old can empty all the wastebaskets into the big trash, help set and clear the table, and make her own bed. A four-year-old can gather laundry, help empty the dishwasher, bring groceries in, etc. The particular chores you assign your children are really unimportant. What is important is that they are learning to be helping members of the family. Paying your child for chores is personal preference. We do not pay our children for regular, weekly chores, as we desire to teach them the value of pitching in for the good of the whole family, not just for personal gain. We want them to develop a unified, team mindset.

Ideas for School-Aged Children

Older children who attend school will automatically have a structured routine. Actually, you may have trouble working free time into their busy schedules! Homework, after-school activities and lessons, and chores usually keep school-aged children so busy that we must work diligently to protect family time. Many families run from school to dance lessons to soccer practice to gymnastics, leaving just enough time in between to zip through a drive-through for a not-so-nutritious dinner. If this describes your family, you may want to re-evaluate your family's activities. Having too many involvements is not in the best interest of the child, or the family as a whole. Children need down time. They need to rest. They need time at home with their family.

Contrary to popular belief, home-schooled children are not the exception to busy schedules. Often, moms will justify overcommitting their home-schooled children to activities outside the home because they are home all day for school. As you consider whether activities have enslaved your family, robbing you of precious bonding time, try weighing mealtime togetherness. If your family is incapable of sharing dinner together at least three nights a week, it could be that individual activities have taken priority over family togetherness. If this is the case, I encourage you to write down the family schedule and evaluate it with your husband. Consider which activities can be eliminated in order to secure quality family time. You may require your children to pick one activity that means the most to them and drop the rest. If they have great passion for more than one, consider rotating seasons for each one.

Whether children attend school or not, find a hobby that can be nurtured at home to cut back on being on the road so much. My son took an interest in beaded necklaces, sported by many of the fellows in our area. We found a kit at Wal-Mart complete with everything one needs to make a variety of beaded necklaces. For the past several months he has enjoyed making all sorts of necklaces for himself, family and friends. He is also intrigued by drums, much to my dismay <grin>. My husband felt that we needed to enhance his musical inclinations, so Wesley got a drum set for his birthday. Because we want our home to be a place where dreams are nurtured, we purchased a beginner's drum video rather than signing him up for weekly drum lessons. We have a small television set up beside his drums so that he can play along with the instructor. Actually, he is banging away right now while I am resisting the urge to rush in, grab the sticks, and break them over my leg. I am choosing to nurture his dreams. Tylenol helps.

My daughter is interested in singing and baking. In order to nurture her dreams and interests at home, we purchased a couple of instrumental soundtracks that come with written lyrics. She organizes "shows" and sells tickets for this grand living-room event. Tickets include popcorn and all seats are front row. To encourage her baking interest, she has a child's easy-bake oven from which we all enjoy the most scrumptious sugar cookies in Alabama!

Keep Some Structure During Summer

With the exception of areas that have gone to year-round school, summer is a time for children to kick off their shoes, relax, and play.

However, structure is still beneficial for preventing whiney, bored, and discontent children. Our schedule is much lighter and much less detailed in the summer, but I still require a few planned activities, lest they become lazy and overly dependent on entertainment. My son had the following summer schedule hanging in his room when he was nine:

Monday

Make bed
Dress / brush teeth
Breakfast
Devotion & memory verse
Cut grass before lunch
Reading time—30 minutes
Game of choice with Alex
Room time—1 hour

Tuesday

Make bed
Dress/ brush teeth
Breakfast
Devotion & memory verse
Play outside—At least 1 hour
Reading time—30 minutes
Vacuum
Room time—1 hour

Wednesday

Make bed
Dress / brush teeth

Breakfast

Devotion & memory verse

Play outside—At least 1 hour

Reading time—30 minutes

Game of choice with Alex

Sweep garage

Room time—1 hour

Thursday

Make bed

Dress/brush teeth

Go to work with Dad (6:00AM—2:00PM)

Room time—1 hour

Friday

Take sheets off bed

Dress / brush teeth

Breakfast

Devotion & memory verse

Play outside—1 hour

Clean house (tubs and toilets, vacuum all carpets)

Reading time—30 minutes

To remind Wesley that his attitude was as important as his action, Philippians 2:14 adorned the top of the schedule: "Do everything without complaining and arguing."

Remember, how you build order into your home is not important. Working out a plan that brings peace and order to your home is. While this was our basic plan for each day, there were many, many summer days where we tossed all responsibilities to the wind, took off to the pool, went to a friend's house, or had a gang of friends over to play. Be flexible. A structured routine does not mean sweeping all spontaneity under the rug. It simply builds a foundation of order as we balance our spontaneous adventures and responsibilities.

You may have noticed that I listed things like making the bed, dressing, and brushing teeth on Wesley's schedule. While this may seem unnecessary, it holds my children accountable for being responsible without my nagging. Our goal is that they learn to take ownership for responsibilities without being told. My daughter struggles with initiating responsibility without reminders. When she "forgets" to make her bed, I wait until she is about to enjoy some free time to say, "Do you have the freedom to watch a video? Have you been responsible today?" She is then required to make her bed, and she loses the freedom of watching a video.

Another helpful hint is to go over the plan for the day during breakfast. Letting your children know that they have a haircut appointment that afternoon or that there will be a trip to the grocery store, shows respect for them and allows them to mentally prepare, rather than being caught off guard on the spur of the moment.

If this chapter seemed overwhelming to you, please keep in mind that none of these suggestions are biblical commands and you are not obligated to do any of them. In fact, if you feel an urgency to implement many of these ideas into your child's daily routine, please check your heart first. There is a danger in putting too much hope in a good routine. Hope and dependence on anything other than Christ will surely lead to failure. Jesus is the giver of peace. No man-made plan can take his place. Ask Jesus for wisdom and walk in confidence that he will guide you. You do not work for the schedule, the schedule works for you. Be flexible when necessary and be sensitive to God's priorities, remembering that Jesus has a plan for each day. You wouldn't want yours to get in the way.

On the other hand, if this chapter has opened your eyes to the beauty and benefits of a structured routine, but you're afraid the change will not be well received, don't bombard your children with too much structure at one time. It could exasperate them to go from little or no structure to large amounts of structure. Add one or two things at a time, slowly establishing a satisfying routine that will not only build character in your children, but will also bring peace, order, and balance to your home.

Nineteen

Keeping Your Home Clean and Organized

WHILE THIS CHAPTER IS INTENDED for those who need a little help getting motivated and organized, I must first address those who suffer from OCCD (Obsessive Compulsive Cleaning Disorder). It is with great sympathy that I confront this issue as I suffer with it myself. Friends and family often complain that they can't set their drinks down without fear of losing them to the dishwasher before they are finished. I normally have two or three cups of coffee each morning. I typically wind up using two or three spoons to add sugar because I put each one in the dishwasher without thinking. My husband says, "If I ever get up in the middle of the night to use the bathroom, the bed's made by the time I get back!"

I do believe this disorder is inherited. My mother had a worse case than I did before she surrendered her cleaning obsessions to the Lord. Wanna know how bad this disorder can get? Mother used to rake her carpet. Yes, you read it right. She would rake her carpet to cover the vacuum tracks and make the fibers all lie in the same direction.

A door-to-door salesman once made the mistake of claiming that my mother's kitchen floor was dirty and could not be cleaned apart from his miracle spray. He pulled out his white hanky with the intention of proving that the floor was actually filthy even though it looked clean. With a knowing chuckle, my dad said, "I'll tell you what, Buddy. If your hanky is anything less than white after you wipe the floor, I'll buy ten bottles of your spray. Bonnie keeps that floor so clean that I would not hesitate to eat off it!" The man dropped to the floor and eagerly rubbed the linoleum with his hanky, determined to make the sale of the day. He left a defeated man.

While some of us need to work on being less obsessed over the cleanliness of the house, others need to give this issue more attention. A faithful keeper of the home will find the balance that is right for her family. She will be reasonable and sober-minded as she "watches over the affairs of her household" (Proverbs 31:27). In other words, she presides over, keeps an eye on, and willingly accepts her position as manager by excelling in her task. Paul acknowledges that it is good for a woman to be "busy at home" (Titus 2:5). The King James Version says women are to be "keepers of the home." Another translation says women are to be "home lovers." A woman who loves her home will be passionately devoted and committed to overseeing the well-being of her household as she faithfully surrenders to her role as "keeper of the home."

Proverbs describes the difference between a wise woman and a foolish woman: "A wise woman builds her house, but with her own hands the foolish one tears hers down" (Proverbs 14:1). A wise woman will build her dream home by thinking, planning, organizing, and laboring. Let us not dread labor. Beautiful rewards and satisfaction come from labor. Sweat and work are not to be despised, as they bring enjoyable results. Cleanliness and order enhance the environment of our homes and surround our loved ones with comfort. This makes the labor of our hands worth the effort.

The woman talked about in Proverbs 31 takes the cake when it comes to managing the home. It's easy to become frustrated by her super-woman characteristics. After all, while she is grasping the spindle with her fingers and opening her arms to the poor before daybreak, many of us are still slapping the snooze button on the alarm clock. I've heard some frustrated women downplay the example of the Proverbs 31 Woman saying, "No wonder she could accomplish so much! The woman had servants!" It has not escaped my attention that she had a little help. The Scriptures are clear that Wonder Woman had servants. "She gets up while it is still dark; she provides food for her family and portions for her servant girls" (Proverbs 31:15). However, we have servants today as well. We have dishwashers, washing machines, and microwaves that do much of the work for us. When we consider our means, we have much to be thankful for.

I must emphasize that there is no one way to run a household. My purpose for giving the following tips is not to make you feel like a failure, frustrate you with guilt, overwhelm you with unrealistic ideas, or cause you to question your own methods, but rather to offer suggestions that might prove beneficial for those who desire a fresh plan of action. Some of these ideas may appeal to you and some may not. That's okay. You are the queen of your castle and the one to determine how it operates best. Sift through this information, weeding out what doesn't apply and planting into your routine what will nurture your home to fruitfulness.

I've said it before and I'll say it again. The following suggestions are not biblical commands. Some of you probably read this chapter title and the air deflated from your balloon. You glanced over at the pile of laundry on the floor and crusty dishes in the sink and were tempted to skip over this chapter to avoid a self-induced guilt trip. Self-induced is a good word. God is not more pleased with you when your home is clean and organized. God is pleased with you because Jesus lives in you. He does not measure your worthiness by your efforts and successes, but by the death and resurrection of his

Son. When your home is not cleaned and organized, God does not condemn you.

Are we to condemn ourselves or accept the condemnation of others because of our weaknesses and failures? Certainly not. We stand before God justified by the blood of Christ. We cast our weaknesses and failures at the foot of the cross; we don't carry them around with us lest they weigh us down with guilt. When we fail, we repent. We lay our burdens down and seek the strength of Jesus to help us grow in holiness.

After reading many books chock full of good homemaking ideas, I have been guilty of thinking *Great! Now I have to do that!* However, I don't have to "do" anything to be a better wife and mom. Because Christ lives in me, I am being transformed, even in the midst of my weaknesses, to be more like Christ. Because Christ lives in me, I don't have to depend on homemaking success for my acceptance and worth. My hope is in Christ who empowers me with the confidence that I have been made perfect, whether my home is clean or not.

Having said all that, it almost seems inappropriate to offer suggestions for keeping your home clean and organized. However, I am confident that by now you understand the difference between biblical mandates and mere suggestions, so I offer the following ideas for the practical side of homemaking.

Have a plan for keeping your home clean

Cleaning the home can be overwhelming without a plan of action. Dirty dishes, piles of laundry, and rings around the tub are like dark, threatening clouds looming over you. There's no need to be enslaved by the chores of daily life. A plan puts you in control. A cleaning routine can set you free. Routine enables you to tackle daily chores and maintenance and enjoy a clean, organized home life. Here are a few ideas that might help you develop your own system:

Weekly cleaning. Have a set day to clean your house and plan on staying home that day. It can be too much to schedule errands on your cleaning day. To get it over with quickly, avoid answering the phone, emails, or anything else that might keep you from completing your cleaning in a timely fashion. Work hard and fast so that it doesn't drag on all day. If cleaning your house in one day seems overwhelming, consider dividing it into two days. I would suggest doing all the scrubbing one day (kitchen and bathrooms) and saving the sweeping, mopping, vacuuming, and dusting for the next day. Avoid stretching it out over more than two days or you may feel like you are always cleaning your house. Keep in mind, your cleaning day(s) will not be overwhelming if your home is kept orderly. Cleaning is frustrating and often avoided if clutter has to be moved first. Order makes for a more welcoming cleaning environment.

If your family members are reasonably neat, you might get away with thorough cleaning one week and spot cleaning the next. To spot clean, simply walk through your home with a bottle of Windex and paper towels, only wiping what needs your attention (splattered mirrors, food in microwave, counters, toilet seats, etc.) Next, sweep, vacuum, and top dust (not moving anything—just a quick, surface dust job). If done quickly, a "walk through" should only take about 30 minutes, and your home is good to go for another week.

Laundry. Plan to do laundry on a different day than cleaning. If possible, do all the laundry in one day. If that seems like too much, do clothes one day and towels and sheets the next. Have a rule that the laundry is to be folded and put away as soon as the timer goes off. Wrinkles and much ironing can be eliminated if clothes are hung or folded hot out of the dryer. Besides, walking past piles of wrinkled laundry that beckons to be put away is frustrating. It takes approximately seven minutes to fold a load of clothes.

Assign chores for your children. Begin teaching children at a young age how to help maintain the home. Work alongside your children until they can do assignments on their own. My children are eleven and eight. On house-cleaning days the chores are divided accordingly:

> **Mom**—clean kitchen, sweep and mop all floors, dust all furniture.
>
> **Wesley** *(eleven)*—clean toilets and tubs in all three bathrooms, vacuum all carpets.
>
> **Alex** *(eight)*—clean sinks, counters, and mirrors in all bathrooms, empty all trashcans into big trash.

By breaking down the housecleaning among family members, it's not overwhelming for anyone. We live in a four-bedroom, three-bathroom home. When everyone works as a team our home is fresh and clean within 1½ hours. Also, when children are responsible for some of the cleaning, they naturally become more sensitive to leaving messes. By helping, they take ownership of the cleanliness of the home and learn to serve as a team. Expecting children to help out around the house beginning at a young age helps prevent bad attitudes about it later. When helping out is something they have grown up doing, objecting or having a bad attitude is less likely to be an issue. For a more cheerful cleaning-day environment, consider playing music while you work together.

Deep clean twice a year. Set goals for unusual chores by scheduling them on your calendar. Chores might include: cleaning baseboards, washing windows, light fixtures, and blinds, and dusting fans and hard-to-reach furniture. By penciling them in on your calendar, they are more likely to get done. However, don't be a slave to your calendar. If something comes up, simply move the chore to another day.

Have a plan for keeping your home organized

The best way to keep an organized home is to abide by the "have a place for everything and keep everything in its place" rule. Without this, it'll never happen. By putting items away when finished, you eliminate clutter before it ever begins. There is never an overwhelming mess when things are kept where they go rather than set aside.

I like to walk through the house before turning in at night to make sure that things are tidy. Waking up in the morning to dirty dishes in the sink and a messy house is depressing. It starts the day with an "it never ends" mentality. Take a few minutes to tidy things up before going to bed and start fresh each morning with a clean, orderly home. It's a good feeling for you as well as your family. Here are a few helpful tips:

Go through mail daily. Don't allow mounds and mounds of mail to pile up. Go ahead and sift through the mail as it arrives, placing pieces that need your attention in a designated area and throwing away junk mail.

Limit toys. If your child has too many toys to keep organized, consider sorting through them. Have your child fill a toy box, toy shelves, or an organized toy closet with their favorites and consider giving or putting the rest away.

Limit clothes. If drawer space and closets are not sufficient to hold all the clothes neatly, weed out clothes that are not being worn. Avoid having different seasons of clothes in the closets and drawers. Put your children's seasonal clothes, that can be tried on again next year, in a box labeled spring/summer or fall/winter and store them in a closet or attic, while placing items that are too small or worn in a giveaway box. If you are a packrat who has a hard time getting rid of your own clothes, consider a "trial closet." Place the items that you never wear but can't seem to part with in this trial closet (or box) so that they are out of sight. If you haven't missed them in one year, give them away. Anything that you can go a year without, you don't need. Good Will Stores take clothes as well as toys, or you might consider a consignment store where you can exchange unwanted items for cash.

Reorganize rooms twice a year. Consider reorganizing one room a week, twice a year, getting rid of items no longer needed. Wal-Mart sells inexpensive plastic organizers in all shapes and sizes. My daughter has a very small bedroom. For organizing toys and clothes she only had one chest of drawers and two small closets. I organized her things by purchasing large, stackable drawers to fill one of the closets. She now has one closet with drawers galore for her toys and personal items and one closet just for clothes. Two of her drawers are actually empty! I also purchased small stackable drawers (plastic and inexpensive) to organize her hair accessories and jewelry. What a difference organizers make!

Limited kitchen space can seem expanded with organizers such as lazy susans in the cabinets and free-standing wire shelves in the pantry for more stacking space.

Keeping Your Motive Christ-Centered

Because this book is sprinkled with practical tips, I am compelled to caution you once again. Please reflect deeply on these next few paragraphs as I believe they are the most important in the book. There are many of us with a natural bent toward being orderly and structured. Perhaps you have read through many of the ideas and tips with a sigh of relief, as routine and order are effectively being implemented in your home. I ashamedly admit that I have been guilty of observing someone else's disorganized home, breathing a self-righteous sigh of relief and smugly thinking, "I do a pretty good job as keeper of the home." This sort of comparative thinking is wrong. Paul warns, "We do not dare classify or compare ourselves with some who commend themselves. When they measure themselves by themselves and compare themselves with themselves, they are not wise" (2 Corinthians 10:12). Our redemption and our identity are not measured by human standards or human comparisons, but rather by Christ, who has covered our ever present inadequacies through his work at Calvary.

Self-reliance presents a great danger. Having a clean, organized home does not make for a more righteous or a godlier woman. To think that it does is to glory in oneself and one's own ability rather than in Christ alone. It's to suggest that somehow our barometer of holiness and perhaps even our salvation are measured by our own achievements. It's tempting for those of us who feel we stay on top of things to place our value and worth in our daily accomplishments, but this misconception substitutes self-reliance for God's grace. A good indicator that our happiness and satisfaction are wrapped up in self-reliance is how we feel when self-performance fluctuates. In other words, when we have a productive day, our confidence soars; when we do not have a productive day, it dwindles and brings us down emotionally. Our confidence should not be staked in who we are and what we have done, but in who Christ is and what he has done. To place our own abilities and accomplishments as the determinant of our worth is to place an idol between us and God. It's to base our salvation on ourselves and our own performances, rather than on the redemptive power of the gospel and the blood of Jesus Christ.

On the other hand, there are many of us with a natural bent toward being disorderly and unstructured. Perhaps the practical tips in this book seem overwhelming and unachievable. Perhaps you enter the home of others and feel defeated, thinking, "If I could only keep house like so-and-so. She always has it together. I'll never be as good as she is." While this is the opposite extreme, it still makes a man-made ideal an idol. To proclaim oneself a failure by lack of achievement is to assume that achievement is our means of approval. Again, our approval is not in our own abilities and accomplishments, or lack thereof, but in the acceptance and atonement of Christ. It has nothing to do with the work we do or don't do, but the work that Jesus did and continues to do in and through us.

Whether we are over-achieving and feel victorious with a bent toward pride, or under-achieving and feel defeated with a bent toward self-pity is not what matters most. What matters most is that we *fully acknowledge* ourselves as sinners in need of God's grace, and that we *fully accept* that our salvation, our righteousness, and our hope are based solely on the Son of God.

Twenty

Demonstrating Hospitality

I SAVED THIS CHAPTER UNTIL LAST because I thought it would be the easiest to write. Over the past couple of months I have jotted down different ways that I demonstrate hospitality, hoping to compile a clever list of ideas for you to draw from. After spending a painfully sweet morning studying what God's Word says about hospitality, my list went in the trash and I went on my knees. I've always considered myself a hospitable gal. After all, I was born and raised in the South. However, after pouring over the Scriptures and seeking God's purpose for hospitality, I have been deeply convicted. He has shown me that what I've been doing is entertaining, and there is a big difference between entertaining and hospitality. This chapter is written from my newly transformed heart when it comes to this issue, not from my personal experience. I will be learning, confessing, and growing to be more like Jesus with every word I write. Please take my hand, and let's walk through this journey to Christ-centered hospitality together and discover how practicing biblical hospitality contributes to heaven at home.

Home: A place for ministering, not entertaining

True hospitality is not found in the pages of *Southern Living*, *Better Homes and Gardens*, or *Good Housekeeping*, but in the Word of God.

Unfortunately, these magazines have distorted the meaning of biblical hospitality by appealing to the lust of the eyes, the lust of the flesh, and the pride of life. We drool over pictures of elaborate homes decorated to perfection and become dissatisfied with our own. We conclude that our homes will never measure up and are not worthy of guests. What we need to realize is that hospitality has nothing to do with things, and everything to do with Christ. It's about obeying him by serving others. Paul wrote that we are to "serve one another in love" (Galatians 5:13b). No matter what talents God has granted us, we are all commanded to "practice hospitality" (Romans 12:13). When we obey, God can use us to touch the hearts of others in ways that we can't even imagine. In her book *Open Heart, Open Home*, Karen Burton Mains writes, "[Hospitality] is a supernatural ministry which, when combined with righteous living, bathed in prayer, and dedicated to the Lord, can be used by God far beyond anything we could ask or think."[1]

Pride often stands in the way of giving ourselves fully to biblical hospitality for the glory of God. Pride entertains people, while hospitality makes them feel welcomed and wanted. My friend Toma demonstrates biblical hospitality like no one else I know. Hers is a home where it's okay to drop in unexpectedly. It's a place where guests can loosen their ties, kick off their shoes, brew their own cup of coffee, and curl their feet under them on the couch.

Toma opened her heart and home to me and loved me during a time that I was not so lovable. Before I knew Christ, I didn't care to be around Christians. My parents were saved in mid-life and forced me to begin attending church at the age of seventeen. I rebelled. I hated church, I disliked the people in the church, and I had grown sick of hearing about God. It was a confusing, difficult, and extremely stressful time in my life. God was calling me and I was running. It was a rough position to be in. Interestingly, when I needed to rest my mind and get away from my parents, I would go to Toma's house (her husband, Cliff, was the one who led my parents to the Lord).

I can remember storming out of my house several times after heated arguments with my parents and heading straight for Toma's. There was rest in Toma's home. I was welcome and accepted. I remember one time in particular when I barged in angry and crying. I didn't want to talk, just calm down and rest. I lay down on her couch, my body convulsing with sobs, as she gently rubbed my back and hummed while I cried myself to sleep.

There was nothing impressive about Toma's house by worldly standards, but to me it was a refuge of comfort and peace. A place where I was welcomed, wanted, and loved. Although I did not know God, there was no doubt in my mind that he dwelled in Toma's house. He used her open heart and open home to reveal himself to me. As a result, a rebellious, promiscuous, alcohol-abusing teenager realized and accepted the love of God. That's what hospitality is all about.

As the wife of a minister and home-schooling mother of five, Toma's mission statement has been, "Do what you can, where you are, with what you have." For many years, she and her husband raised four children in a 1500-square-foot, three-bedroom, two-bathroom home. They welcomed hundreds and hundreds of people into these small living quarters. Their home was so full of love that it was never too small to receive college students for Bible study, missionaries who needed to rest, and people who just needed to come and be loved. The Scriptures say that when we are faithful with a little, God entrusts us with more (Luke 16:10). When Cliff and Toma had their fifth child, God blessed them with a much larger home. To this day, they remain faithful to open their hearts and home regularly to any who will come.

Hospitality is not about impressing others with our clever decorating, gourmet cooking, or clean and organized homes. It's about welcoming, serving, and loving people in the name of Jesus and for the sake of the gospel. It's about an attitude of willingness to be used by God at all times in all ways, not just when it's convenient. Paul said it's about sharing our lives: "We loved you so much that we were delighted to share with you not only the gospel of God but our lives as well, because you have become so dear to us" (1 Thessalonians 2:8). The gospel is presented through our lives, not just our words. Sharing our homes is sharing our lives. One of the main differences between entertainment and hospitality is that entertainment focuses on things (condition of house, food, convenience, etc.), while hospitality focuses on people. Hospitality is not so much an act as it is an attitude of otherness. Here are some defining differences of attitude between the two:

Entertaining says, "We can't have the pastor's family over tonight! I didn't cook. I had just planned on having grilled cheese sandwiches and soup!"

Hospitality says, "Let's have the pastor's family over for grilled cheese sandwiches and soup. We haven't fellowshipped with them in a while."

Entertaining says, "I'll start having company when I move into a bigger house and replace the living room furniture."

Hospitality says, "I will honor the Lord with what he has given me by opening my home to you."

Entertaining says, "I want to impress you with my beautiful home and my cooking talents. My home is a reflection of who I am."

Hospitality says, "My home is a gift from God. I want to use it for his purpose and reflect his love by welcoming and serving you."

Entertaining says, "The missionaries can't stay at my house. I haven't finished decorating the guest bedroom."

Hospitality says, "Although the room is not decorated, I'll prepare a place for you in my home anytime."

Entertaining thrives on words of approval and a pat on the back: "You are a remarkable hostess!" or "You have impeccable taste!"

Hospitality focuses on others and the details of their lives, not on cooking the perfect meal and having the house spotless.

Entertaining is "put out" when guests are late and aggravated by being inconvenienced.

Hospitality puts others first by being gracious, understanding, and flexible.

Entertaining leads to pride and terrible bondage. It is a rigorous taskmaster that enslaves.

Hospitality offers liberating freedom to minister at any time.

So many of us have moved away from biblical hospitality. In today's busy world, we claim our possessions and time as our own. We can learn much from the book of Acts where believers lived the biblical model: "All believers were one in heart and mind. No one claimed that any of his possessions was his own, but they shared everything they had" (Acts 4:32). With this mindset we would welcome guests no matter what. We would welcome folks who drop in unexpectedly with open arms without embarrassing them with comments such as, "I'm sorry the house is so messy." We would welcome our children's friends even though the carpets might get stained. We would welcome every opportunity to open our homes for the purpose of glorifying God and making an eternal difference in someone's life.

When we insist on having the table set perfectly, the house immaculate, and everything just so every time we have company, we don't allow people to see us as we really are. People will feel more welcomed if things are laid back and less formal. Some of the best fellowships I've experienced were at Toma's house where there were so many people that we had to eat on bamboo lap trays while sitting on the floor. What made it special was that the focus was on us, not the meal or the details. Toma never complained that she didn't have enough chairs or real plates for her guests. She never apologized that we had to sit on the floor. Those things didn't matter to her or us. What mattered was that we were invited, welcomed, and loved. That's hospitality at its finest!

Guests feel less like awkward strangers in our homes and more like family when we allow them to help out by putting ice in the glasses, setting the table, or buttering the rolls. Allowing them to help puts them at ease, makes them feel a part of our home, and overcomes possible intimidation. We should be careful not to hide behind the façade of perfectionism, but let people see us as we are. We need to relax and not be so concerned with cleaning, preparing the table, and having everything so perfect that we are distracted from ministering, which is God's intention for true hospitality.

We must also remember that hospitality does not have to involve a meal. Inviting someone for coffee or dessert lends opportunities to minister when time is limited or finances are tight. One friend keeps leftover homemade cake and store bought pies in the freezer for guests she invites over spur-of-the-moment. When we consider a biblical view of hospitality, we are without excuse to honor and obey the Lord when it comes to opening our hearts and homes to others.

We are to demonstrate hospitality not only to our friends and family. With friends and family we get something back, whether it be preferred fellowship or a return invitation to their house. It is good to fellowship with friends and family. However, God blesses us more when we are willing to fellowship and serve those who may not be on our preferred guest lists. Not only can he use us to make an eternal difference in someone's life, but giving up our own agenda and following his will can make an eternal difference in our own lives as well. The book of Luke records a time when Jesus shared a meal with a prominent Pharisee: "Then Jesus said to his host, 'When you give a luncheon or dinner, do not invite your friends, your brothers or relatives, or your rich neighbors; if you do, they may invite you back and so you will be repaid. But when you give a banquet, invite the poor, the crippled, the lame, the blind, and you will be blessed. Although they cannot repay you, you will be repaid at the resurrection of the righteous.'" (Luke 14:12–14). Are we about the Father's business?

Modeling hospitality for our children

Hospitality does everything with no thought of reward, but takes pleasure in the joy of giving, doing, loving, and serving for the glory of God, not just for acquaintances but also for our families. Our homes must be a welcoming refuge for our husbands and children before they can become a welcoming refuge for others. Hospitality counts for nothing if we are rude and ugly to our children while preparing for the arrival of company. We should speak to our children the same way we speak to friends, with courtesy and respect, lest they see hypocrisy in our lives. They will look forward to company coming if our attitudes are truly ones of service. On the other hand, if we are stressed out and irritable, "hospitality" will become something they dread.

It benefits our children when we involve them in hospitality. They shouldn't be shooed from the room as if they are less important than guests. When children live in a hospitable home they learn to be hospitable. Allow them to answer the door and greet the guests, take their coats, help fill the glasses, clear the table, play with younger children, and offer their bedrooms for overnight guests. When possible, allow them to sit at the table and be a part of the fellowship. We shouldn't overlook our children in the process of ministering to others, but have them minister alongside us, watching and learning. We should be careful of what we say and how we say it, tempering our commands with kindness, and not using our children as the brunt of jokes.

We can teach them hospitality by not getting upset when they or their friends accidentally spill something or track mud on the floor. Allowing neighborhood kids in to have a glass of water or use the bathroom are simple ways of showing hospitality. Little eyes are watching, little ears are listening, little minds are processing, and little hearts are learning what it means to serve others and demonstrate the love of Christ in relation to hospitality. May we take that responsibility seriously that we might be good parents, wise teachers, and faithful servants of God. May our homes be little oases of hospitality to a people often shunted aside by the busyness that plagues our society. And may we offer a glimpse of the glorious eternity that Christ has prepared for us as we share *heaven at home* with family, friends, and wandering sheep.

Conclusion

As A LITTLE GIRL I enjoyed spending the night with friends . . . for about two hours, then I longed for home. After a while at my friend's house, visions of my family, gathered in the living room in cozy pajamas, my mama offering freshly made Rice Krispy treats, my daddy scanning the television channels for a good family flick, and my brother sprawled on the floor working on his latest Lego invention, danced in my head. Once the visions set in, nothing but home would do. No amount of begging and pleading from my friend could change my mind. The longer I waited to call my daddy, the more intense my longing for home became, until finally my whole being ached to be there. When I finally picked up the phone and called my daddy to come get me, I broke down in sobs as his familiar voice soothed, "It's okay, Sugar."

He never seemed "put out" or angry that I wanted to come home, but always assured me that he would come get me. He sounded as though he *wanted* to bring me home and calm my insecurities. When the doorbell rang, my heart leaped, and as the door opened and my daddy's frame came into view, comfort and assurance washed over me. As I melted in the safety of my daddy's arms, I silently agreed with Dorothy that yes, indeed, there's no place like home.

Our heavenly Father comes for us when we call. In Romans we are assured that he will not reject the call: "Everyone who calls on the name of the Lord will be saved" (Romans 10:13). He'll never answer those who cry out to him with anger or condemnation, but with welcoming arms opened wide. How do we call on him? The Bible explains that it's by putting our trust in him through belief and confession: "That if you confess with your mouth, 'Jesus is Lord,' and believe in your heart that God raised him from the dead, you will be saved. For it is with your heart that you believe and are justified, and it is with your mouth that you confess and are saved. As the Scripture says, 'Anyone who trusts in him will never be put to shame.'" (Romans 10: 9–11).

Jesus has prepared a home for us in Heaven and delights in the day that he will come and get us. Mark explains that day, "At that time men will see the Son of Man coming in the clouds with great power and glory. And he will send his angels and gather the elect from the four winds, from the ends of the earth to the ends of the heavens" (Mark 13:26–27). In the book of John, Jesus speaks of the home he has prepared for his beloved; the home he will take us to when he comes to get us: "In my Father's house are many rooms; if it were not so, I would have told you. I am going there to prepare a place for you. And if I go and prepare a place for you, I will come back and take you to be with me that you also may be where I am" (John 14: 2–3). Oh, how I long to be in my Father's house!

While the goal of this book is how to establish heaven at home, because of sin our earthly homes can never reflect the splendor and majesty of God's eternal heaven. No matter how heavenly home may be, it pales in comparison to the glorious home he has built for us in glory, where our tears are wiped away and our disgraces removed (Isaiah 25:8). Matthew Henry said, "Earth is embittered to us, that Heaven may be endured."[1] However, because of God's grace and the outpouring of the Holy Spirit in and through us, slices of heaven can certainly enhance our homes.

While this book contains many practical ideas for balancing our responsibilities as wives and mothers, pursuing right relationships, and being effective keepers of the home, a peaceful home is measured by the extent to which Christ reigns. In other words, the less there is of us and the more there is of Christ, the more heavenly home will be.

Endnotes

Chapter One

1. Randy Alcorn, *In Light of Eternity* (Colorado Springs: Waterbrook Press, 1999), 31–32.

Chapter Three

1. Lysa Terkeurst, *Capture His Heart* (Chicago: Moody Press, 2002), 94–96.

Chapter Four

1. Ginger Plowman, *Don't Make Me Count to Three!* (Wapwallopen: Shepherd Press, 2004), 19–21.
2. Robert C. Crosby, *Now We're Talking! Questions That Bring You Closer to Your Kids* (Colorado Springs: Focus on the Family, 1996), xii.

Chapter Five

1. Linda Dillow & Lorraine Pintus, *Intimate Issues* (Colorado Springs: Waterbrook Press, 1999), xi.
2. Ibid., 9–10.

Chapter Seven

1. Ginger Plowman, *Don't Make Me Count To Three,* (Wapwallopen: Shepherd Press, 2004), 57.
2. Ken Sande, *The Peacemaker,* (Grand Rapids: Baker Books, 1991), 76.

Chapter Nine

1. Words and Music, *Helen H. Lemmel,* 1922.
2. Frank C. Houghton, *Amy Carmichael of Dohnavur* (London: Hobber & Stoughton, 1974), 250.
3. C.S. Lewis, *Mere Christianity* (London: Fontana, 1952), 113–114.
4. Hazel Felleman, *The Best Loved Poems of the American People* (Garden City: Garden City Books, 1936), 364.

Chapter Ten

1. www.motherinlawstories.com
2. Spiros Zodhiates Th.D., *The Complete Word Study Dictionary* (Chattanooga: AMG Publishers, 1992), 1447.

Chapter Eleven

1. Elizabeth George, *Life Management for Busy Women* (Eugene: Harvest House Publishers, 2002), 159.

Chapter Twelve

1. Ginger Plowman, *Don't Male Me Count to Three,* (Wapwallopen: Shepherd Press, 2004), 141–145.

Chapter Thirteen

1. Ibid., 147–151.

Chapter Twenty

1. Karen Burton Mains, *Open Heart, Open Home,* (Elgin: David C. Cook Publishing Co., 1976), 13.

Conclusion

1. Matthew Henry, *Zondervan NIV Matthew Henry Commentary,* (Grand Rapids: Zondervan Publishing House, 1992), 289.